My Island

The true story of a silent challenge

My Island

The true story of a silent challenge

Maggie Gordon

Illustrated by Hamish Rosie

1999

The Orcadian Limited (Kirkwall Press)

Published by The Orcadian Limited (Kirkwall Press),
Hell's Half Acre, Hatston, Kirkwall, Orkney, Scotland, KW15 1DW
Tel.: 01856 879000   Fax: 01856 879001

ISBN 0 9526174 9 8

Printed by The Orcadian Limited, Print Centre,
Hell's Half Acre, Kirkwall, Orkney, Scotland

Dedication

The illustrations are for my mother,
and the text is for my father

Contents

Foreword

I first met Hamish Rosie on a summer's evening in 1996 when he accompanied Maggie Gordon and her husband Bob on a visit to our home in the Borders.

I had previously met Maggie and Bob a few years earlier, during 1992, when in somewhat different circumstances, we had the small matter of a house sale to attend to. They were moving back south to Brighton at that time, while I was beginning the process of looking for a new place to stay. I came out to view the property and discovered, to my surprise, that they were both graphic designers, working from a studio at the house. We immediately struck up a rapport, my own occupation back in the days before music took over, was indeed the very same. (A quick demonstration of Apple Mac and Quark design systems soon put any stray thoughts I might have harboured about re-visiting the old job, firmly back where they came from.) Things had moved on a bit! Anyway, the studio was going to be just right for making music.

This time though, it was an entirely social visit. They had arrived back from a visit to South Ronaldsay in the Orkney Islands and I can remember Maggie, brimming with enthusiasm. It had been her very first visit there and I could tell that the island had made a big impression. She was planning to write a book, and the main purpose of the Orkney trip was to do some research and take in the island's life and atmosphere. I was intrigued – was this to be a book about the island itself, an historical account or a novel, perhaps? Their friend, Hamish, had remained silent up until this point, but now *he* was telling me, leaving me in no doubt, exactly what the book was going to be about. The sunshine outdoors had become a warm ray of light inside as he articulated, in his own very personal way . . . and in a moment, it became so clear and obvious why Maggie had been drawn towards writing this book.

Anyone meeting Hamish for the first time could not fail to be struck by his warmth and humour, and underlying it, bubbling away beneath the surface, this huge well of energy and giving, simply bursting to get out. It's almost as if Maggie had accepted a role as intermediary/interpreter charged with putting his life into words and giving him back a portion of the gifts which he was denied, this manifesting itself in a special friendship with at times, an almost telepathic understanding.

As a musician, I cannot even begin to imagine what it must be like to live in a world without sound. Not only has Hamish had to learn to cope with profound deafness throughout his life, he also, at an early age, was faced with making the enormous decision of leaving his island home in order to receive an appropriate education on the Scottish mainland, or consider the alternative of staying, and the possibility of a more detached existence. He went along with the brave decision to go, applying his patience and determination to overcoming the inevitable difficulties that life would place before him.

But, although the separation was now permanent, in a physical sense, his own spiritual attachment to the island has always remained – throughout his journey, and all the years spent in the south, the island of South Ronaldsay has been his life's touchstone. His own island; a symphony in the sound of the silence.

Islands are special places. Not just simply as home and the place of birth, but so much more. The binding tie of landscapes and the ever-changing light, sea and colour; the people; the language; tradition and history. The experience stays with you, forever a part of your essential being because that is what you are and always will be, after all . . . an islander. Our islands become our places of refuge that we can flee to and feel cocooned from the outside; we feel secure in the knowledge that they are there for us, our own earthly piece of heaven in an often turbulent world. I suppose I write these words as they apply to my own life, also. I spent my early years living on two islands, North Uist and Skye, during the Fifties and Sixties and consider myself fortunate to have experienced some of the last years of the old Gaelic ways, just before the introduction of television and the inevitable cultural erosion. It was a blissful time. The start of my own exile however, began at the age of eighteen, when I left school to go to art school in Glasgow and I guess that hardly a day has gone by since then that I have not referred to the ever-present mantra of returning, this thought in itself being a constant thread running through life and through work.

Perhaps this is what many exiled islanders are fated to be – only able to love and dream from afar. And, also, maybe this is the crux . . . that the very nature of this state is what actually preserves and nourishes the dream. For behind it, lies the awful fear that a permanent return might somehow shatter, and this loss would be much the greater to bear.

For Hamish, then, I am so pleased that this beautiful book about his life has been published at last. And I know how proud and good he feels about it, and how much a labour of love it has been for Maggie. For the rest of us, it is an opportunity to share the experiences and struggles of a fellow traveller on a difficult journey and if we allow ourselves to stop off for a while, to pause, and consider, our own lives will be the richer.

Rory Macdonald
of Runrig, the Gaelic-Rock group
March, 1999

Introduction

As Hamish's biographer, I would like to introduce him to you. He stands almost six foot tall, is solid looking with broad shoulders and greying, brindled, tightly waved hair. He has a kindly demeanour and a habit of stroking his full beard when musing on things. He wears glasses, has lively grey-green eyes and to pass him in the street you would not notice anything unusual about him. But if you were introduced to him you would become aware of him looking intently at you, concentrating on your every facial move as you speak. In his reply to you, his voice would sound very small and his speech unusually different. You would, however, notice his unusually expressive face and eyes. You would have to listen very attentively to catch what he was saying. It is not always easy to understand Hamish at first – he is pre-lingually, profoundly deaf. If you were to talk to him, there would be a few simple rules you could observe to make it easier for him to lip read you: make sure you faced the light, speak a little more slowly than usual and enunciate clearly. Although he has no knowledge or memory of sound there is nothing external to suggest this. He appears as normal as anyone else and has a particularly positive outlook on life. Once you get to know him, you would discover what a direct, genuine and remarkable man he is. His eyes twinkle and his facial expression changes constantly, giving meaning and colour to what he is saying whether spoken or signed. He would instinctively know that you would be far more concerned about following his speech and making yourself understood than he would be about meeting you and would make a great effort to try to put you at your ease. Ask him how he is at more or less any time and he will give the same answer, "Fine," his head on one side, a smile across his bearded face confirming his answer by raising his thumbs in the corresponding sign. Both his deaf and hearing friends often remark, just a touch enviously, " How does Hamish manage to always be so positive?" He does so because he works at it every day of his life. It doesn't simply happen. He is a man of immense discipline and for me an inspiring friend.

I first met Hamish more than twenty five years ago, through my husband, Bob – a graphic designer, who worked with him in the Display Group in the Architect's Department at what was then Greater London Council. Bob would frequently come home from work with tales of this unusual man. I became increasingly fascinated by how he had gradually surmounted the barriers of his total deafness. I was intrigued by his background and the way in which his mother and father had faced the challenge of bringing up their only, profoundly deaf child.

I eventually persuaded Hamish to tell me his story as he remembers it. To start at the beginning, we decided to go back to his Orkney island where the story started and, from there, journey back to the present through the highs and lows, tears and laughter of his determined struggle to make his way in the hearing world. This return to Hamish's roots became the catalyst for *My Island*. Encouraging him to talk about the times which did not always match up to the bright, positive man he now is, probing, questioning and coming to understand the life of this profoundly deaf man, was a challenge for me, as a hearing person. I also had to find the right language to set out for him, what were essentially visual memories. But together we made this journey and *My Island* charts this truly inspiring story.

Maggie Gibson

Acknowledgements

I would like to thank Hamish for sharing his story with me and for putting up with the endless questions and faxes needed to clarify points. Thanks must also go to Morag, Hamish's wife, for her support and advice and all the people who so generously contributed their recollections to this book; in particular Hamish's father, Jim and Vera Doull, Bessie Groat and her family, Billy Banks and Mollie King. Lastly, my thanks go to Bob, my husband, for his patient encouragement and invaluable critical eye.

CHAPTER 1 *Return to Orkney*

I was born in the village of St Margaret's Hope on the Orkney island of South Ronaldsay during the Second World War. My determination to overcome the potential isolation of deafness began there. To bring my story to life for Maggie, who wanted to record it, I took her to see my island for herself. Late in the summer, she and I, together with her husband Bob, drove the length of the British Isles from my home in Surrey, up to the far north coast of Scotland, to catch the ferry across to Orkney. We broke the journey with an overnight stop in the Borders and left early the following morning to allow time to visit Wick, my maternal grandparents' home, before driving up to the port of Scrabster.

We arrived in Wick in the afternoon hoping to find my grandparents' house. I was quite surprised at still being able to remember the way through the town to the little end-of-terrace house where I had spent many wonderful days as a child. We parked the car and I got out and stood on the pavement taking a long look at 9, Willowbank. My mind went back to my grandparents and I thought of how my deafness must have saddened them. Though, as a child, I was never aware of it. I remember my grandmother so well, always busying herself about the house, washing and ironing, cooking and cleaning. She even attempted to get me to do a few small household jobs! Tantalising smells came from her kitchen and the house always had a clean, fresh smell to it. My grandmother was kind and generous and always made a great fuss of me. Looking back, it couldn't have been easy for her or my grandfather to understand me because I had very little language with which to communicate and neither of them knew how to sign. In those days, very few people did. I don't really know how I managed to understand either of them but somehow I did. When my grandmother wanted to talk to me, she would concentrate on helping me to understand a few key words. Once I had them, I could follow the sense of what she was saying.

I crossed the road to the lane that ran down the side of the house to see if the garden was still there. Although it too had changed and the open view out across the harbour had been blocked by new buildings, I could picture it exactly the way it was with the wash house, where my grandmother did the family laundry, and the aviary that my grandfather had built himself. The canaries he bred and showed were his pride and joy. Whenever I visited, he would encourage me to help him prepare their food, following his own special recipe which consisted of a type of crushed, thick biscuits and boiled eggs! My grandfather was a thoughtful, caring man though very different from my grandmother when it came to communicating with me. He relied on pointing and gestures and we learned to understand each other in this way. I would never have been able to lip read him as he was a great pipe smoker and had a fine moustache which

My grandfather in Wick was a canary breeder. He took pride in his birds.

obscured his lip patterns. My grandfather liked to take me into Wick to visit his friends or some of my many cousins who lived in the town. He would take my hand and we would make our way through the streets and he would point out things of particular note or interest. I remember being taken to see two of my cousins who ran their own printing business. I was fascinated by the smell of the paper and printing inks, the printing presses and the different trays of wood and metal type. Little did I know that my future career would involve working closely with printers!

There were other times when he would take me and his dog, Rap, for a walk down to the harbour to watch the boats bring in their catch and then into the fishmarket, where my uncle

Douglas worked. I was intrigued by the bustle, the men in their long, waterproof aprons and big rubber boots heaving large crates around, the different fish lying on beds of ice, the wet slippery floor and the unforgettable smell of it all. I felt very important knowing that my uncle worked there. I so enjoyed these outings with my grandfather – there was always so much to see and so many new and different things to discover.

I brought my mind back to the present and made my way back to the car to rejoin my friends and we left Wick, driving up to Scrabster in the bright afternoon sun to catch the ferry across to Orkney. Today, with the summer weather, the crossing to Stromness would be in stark contrast to the many rough crossings that I had made in the past. Smooth sailings in this area tend to be few and far between, the water separating the islands from the Caithness coast is full of dangerous currents and rarely calm. We joined the queue of cars waiting to be loaded and, once on board, made our way up on to the deck.

On board, I thought back to the time when I travelled to Wick with my mother to visit my grandparents. We made the same crossing that we were doing now – only in reverse and on a steamer called the *St Ola*. It was a great adventure for me. Sailing on a ferry gave me a tremendous thrill and I remember watching the derrick hoisting up the cars and livestock from the same dockside that we had just left, loading them into the hold before we were allowed to board for our journey. I loved the smell of the steam and the smoke that poured out of the tall, black funnel leaving smuts everywhere! Although I couldn't hear the sound of the engine, I could feel the throb and rhythm of it which was very exciting. The feel of the movement of the ship on the water was a wonderful experience for me, particularly when the sea was rough, which it often was. When I think about some of the storms we encountered, I am amazed that the *St Ola* regularly made it to Scrabster. There were times when the seas were so wild that the waves looked as though they would build up to such a height that they would crash right over the boat. The captain would then immediately order passengers and crew alike inside, no one was allowed to remain on deck. When this happened I was always very disappointed – I far preferred standing on deck with the spray, wind and rain lashing my face, holding on to the railings feeling the boat heave up and down – it was so exhilarating and made me feel as though I was at one with the elements. My poor mother never shared my love of the sea or boats. She suffered so seriously from sea sickness, even on relatively smooth crossings, that a berth had to be found for her down below so that she could at least lie down while the sickness raged. I felt so sorry for her. At times like this, she had no choice but to leave me to my own devices even though I was only eight or nine years old. I remember feeling quite surprised at being given this unusual freedom.

The ss St Ola I, very old I can remember. It was terrible when crossing Pentland Firth, one of strongest currents in the world. I often said to myself how did she survive very severe storms. Poor mother, she was very sea sick, as usual!

On this calm evening, we sailed out on the latest *St Ola*, past the most northerly point of Scotland, Dunnet Head, and to the right I could see the outline of South Ronaldsay in the distance as we sailed towards the island of Hoy. I stood for a long time watching the little awks, puffins and cormorants gliding and skimming across the water as we made our way up to the top of Hoy past its spectacular cliffs, the famous Old Man of Hoy and round past the little island of Graemsay. Soon we were approaching Stromness and its harbour where the boat eventually docked. We disembarked and started the final stage of our journey by driving to St Margaret's Hope where we were to stay. It was wonderful to be back in the part of the world that I came from and where my story began.

The mv St Ola, we frequently sailed to Scrabster to visit my grandparents (my mother's parents) in Wick. A lovely boat with beautiful wood panelled interior, I never forgot.

We first drove down to Kirkwall, the capital of Orkney, where I could see the familiar, tall, red sandstone tower and spire of St Magnus Cathedral which seemed strangely small now – it had always seemed so big to me when I was little. It was one of several, personal landmarks I had as a child on the journey between Kirkwall and St Margaret's Hope. This one was particularly symbolic for me – as it was the last significant building that I saw before having to catch the boat back to boarding school in Aberdeen. My parents would drive me down to Kirkwall harbour and once we had passed the spire, I knew I was really leaving home. Seeing it again, brought back memories of the many tearful farewells to my mother and father on the quayside. They would see me safely on to the boat with my suitcase and I would stand out on deck anxiously waiting for them to return to the quayside to wave a last goodbye. As the boat often sailed when it was dark, they would always stand near a street lamp, to ensure that I could see them and I would

St Magnus Cathedral in Kirkwall. I always admired its architecture, built in 1157.

Bye Bye to my parents and our dog Laddie when the boat St Magnus left Kirkwall for Aberdeen - a very sad moment. Naturally I cried!

watch my mother waving her handkerchief until she disappeared out of sight. Those farewells were very hard. I never wanted to go back to school. But by contrast, the return journeys from school for the holidays were full of happy anticipation. As the boat sailed into the harbour in the early morning, I would quickly scan the quayside to locate my parents who, I knew, would always be there waiting to meet me off the boat. As soon as I saw them, I would wave furiously until they saw me and waved back. Once the boat had docked I would make my way down the stairs to get off the boat to be with them as quickly as possible. We would all get into my father's Morris 8 and as the car pulled away from the harbour, I knew I would soon catch sight of the cathedral spire which was the confirmation that I was home again. It was a wonderful feeling of release.

Maggie, Bob and I drove through Kirkwall, and the silhouette of another landmark, the

Highland Park Distillery, came into view. As a child I had no idea what it was but, as far as I was concerned, it remained a memorable shape on the horizon. We continued out into the countryside and past my next landmark which had once been my Aunt Maggie's croft. She is dead now but I remember going to visit her when I was small and the thick smell of burning peat in her hearth making me feel sick. But I did enjoy the marvellous view she had from up there, out over Scapa Flow and the other islands. I used to walk further up the field to see if I could spot the green buoy that marked the place where *HMS Royal Oak* was torpedoed in World War II with the dreadful loss of some 800 lives.

Another landmark coming home – one of Churchill Barriers. Years ago, my father drove his Royal Mail van sometimes through terrible stormy weathers.

When we reached the little village of St Mary's in Holm we came across yet another of my landmarks – the little sub Post Office where many years ago my father, the postman, would call with the mail on his way back from Kirkwall to St Margaret's Hope. On we went until we reached the major landmark of my childhood journey, the first of the four Churchill Barriers across to Lamb Holm where the Italian Chapel stands. I simply knew it as a sort of curved building with a tall thing sticking out of the top (the spire). In time, as I grew up and my understanding developed, I learned what the Highland Park Distillery and the Italian Chapel really were. I learned how the Churchill Barriers were originally constructed during World War II from huge concrete blocks cast by the Italian POW's from the camp on Lamb Holm and how they had ingeniously converted a long Nissen hut into a little chapel. The Barriers were designed to safeguard the British Fleet in Scapa Flow, but now they form a series of causeways that link four of the Orkney islands. They are highly exposed and crossing them in rough weather can be very dangerous. As we drove along the open road of the fourth Barrier, the familiar silhouettes of the great block ships loomed out of the evening sea at strange angles. These were sunk in the narrow channels during both World Wars to prevent entrance to Scapa Flow.

Italian Chapel, another landmark on my way home from boarding school.

Driving on to South Ronaldsay soil gave me the same thrill that I felt when coming home for the school holidays. This was 'my island,' the island that I had told my friends so much about. We passed fertile fields and the old stone house where a long time ago Mrs Pratt, one of my father's 'post' customers, used to live. She had an arrangement with Postman Jackie to leave any letters she had for the post in the window for him to collect on his rounds, and showed her appreciation of this "obligement" by leaving a weekly half dozen, freshly laid hen's eggs on her kitchen table for him to collect with her letters. It never mattered whether she was in or not as

Mrs Pratt put her letter on the front window to tell my father to collect it.

people rarely locked their doors in those days so my father would simply knock and walk in. Seeing Mrs Pratt's old house reminded me of a particular childhood treat. During my school summer holidays when I came back to Orkney from Aberdeen, I would often be allowed to accompany my father on his rounds. I felt very proud sitting beside him in the front of the Royal Mail van and helping him deliver the post. Most of the customers on his rounds got to know me. This meant an added attraction – the occasional treat of home made lemonade or ice cream from one or other of my father's satisfied customers, who always seemed delighted to see their postman's young son 'lending a hand' with the post.

As we came over the brow of the low hill, I leant forward and looked hard into the fading

The lit up kitchen window below the hill is my home.

light of the distance. I could just make out the outline of my childhood home and excitedly pointed it out to my friends. We drove down into St Margaret's Hope to the cottage where we were to stay. It stood on the water's edge looking across the 'Hope itself, up to my birthplace. A little weary and hungry, we parked the car, got out to breathe in the fresh evening air and take in the surroundings. "My *home* – you see the light up the hill, *that's* Hameneuk, my home" I told my friends. We had finally arrived.

After long terms in Aberdeen school, and
arriving at Kirkwall Harbour, we drove home to
St Margaret's Hope, we passed a powerful
silhouette of the building. I never knew what it
was until later. It was Highland Park Distillery
in Kirkwall.

CHAPTER 2 *Hameneuk – my Home*

Hameneuk built by my father. Vera and Jim Dorell, very good friends of ours now live there. Their son is named after me!

It was marvellous to be able to wake up and look out of the cottage window across the bay up to my old home. I had decided to spend time on my own that day, so I got up very early and left the cottage to take a long look at Hameneuk. This small and unassuming hillside house will always have a special place in my thoughts, it is the source of my security and affections even though I spent only the first four years of my life and subsequent school holidays there. It is a unique reminder of my father's unstoppable enterprise and energy. He built Hameneuk almost single handed on a corner plot, hence its name – 'Home in the Corner,' given to him complete with deeds by his boss. This was the first time he had ever undertaken anything on such a large scale, but he was undaunted by limited funds, materials, equipment or technical expertise. Despite the enormity of the task and the frequently adverse weather, he completed his very special wedding present for my mother in just two years.

In order to construct Hameneuk, he first cast a total of two thousand six hundred blocks. He made three wooden four-block moulds, so that batches of a dozen blocks could be cast at a time. Every other morning, before setting off on his post rounds, he would mix up a quantity of cement, fill the moulds and leave the blocks to set. The following morning he would fold down the hinged sides of each mould and carefully extract the hardened concrete blocks, stacking them up ready for transport to his building plot. It took him just over a year to complete all of the blocks at a cost of tuppence ha'penny (one pence) each. He told me it was a real labour of love. All this work was done at the family croft near Herston, a mile or so from his building plot at St Margaret's Hope, so transport for the blocks had somehow to be arranged. He did this quite simply by stopping the coal lorry or anyone else who happened to be driving by and asking them if they would mind dropping off a few blocks on his building plot, in St Margaret's Hope. Nobody ever refused and the entire quantity was delivered in this way!

In the midwinter with snow on the frozen ground and icy winds blowing off the North Sea, my father and a friend finally roofed the house. It was so cold that my father worked wearing two overcoats and thick gloves in a desperate attempt to keep warm. Later in the year, in more clement weather, he laid 'pavements' round the house with big slabs of slate from the

My father made building blocks – 2600 of them. About 12 blocks daily. They were used for constructing Hameneuk a wedding present for my mother – 1936.

9

quarry on Swona, off Caithness. His distant cousin, James Rosie, who lived on the island brought the slabs across by boat to the pier at St Margaret's Hope where he would unload them for collection. The seas around the island of Swona also provided the magnificent redwood joists for the floors of Hameneuk. The wood was salvaged from an American ship shortly after it had been wrecked off the coast of Swona. The shipwrecks around these coasts caused by the fog and very strong tides, often gave up unexpected cargo. My father remembers a time when, at low tide, he walked out to another wreck, lying off the shore of Swona and peered deep down inside to see rows of brand new cars still anchored in the hold. The wreck was a terrible sight, but some enterprising individuals somehow managed to salvage two of the cars and eventually got them up and running.

My father's building of Hameneuk has always impressed me. I learnt a great deal from his resourcefulness and practical skills and over the years I have been able to put much of this into my own life. In the school holidays, I spent hours with him in his workshop, watching his every move as he invented gadgets of all kinds, repaired and built simple radios, and generally fixed and mended a whole range of things. It was an effortless and enjoyable way of learning for me. My father was never at a loss for ideas and always found practical ways of solving problems. Today at ninety one years old, he is as enterprising as ever. For example, I recently took him to visit Maggie where he noticed she had some difficulty in watering some out of reach house plants. A week or so later he had constructed a tipping watering can on the end of a pole made entirely from recycled bits and pieces – an old curtain pole, a marmalade tin, some copper piping and string. It worked perfectly! His ingenuity never fails to astonish me.

My father and mother were very different from each other in character. Perhaps that was what attracted my practical father to the well educated new teacher from Wick who was to take up her position at Tomison's Academy in the South Parish of my island. He and his brother had a car hire business which also ran a taxi service and he was sent to meet her off the boat and drive her up to the South Parish church manse. She was to lodge there with the minister until the repair work on the school house, where the resident teacher normally stayed, was completed.

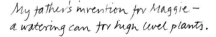

My father's invention for Maggie – a watering can for high level plants.

The Minister was well known for the magic lantern shows he gave in the village hall and my father was in charge of operating the lantern. Inevitably the minister's temporary lodger became a regular member of the audience so my father began to see more and more of her. When she eventually moved away to the school house, my father would visit her on his motorbike.

My parents' friendship grew, their courtship began and my father started to build Hameneuk in anticipation of the future. When they eventually decided to marry, choosing where the wedding should take place presented them with a dilemma. If it were to be on South Ronaldsay, almost the entire population of the island would expect to be invited, and similarly, if they settled on Wick, my mother's home, most of the town would expect to be asked to the ceremony. They both wanted a simple, quiet wedding. So the dilemma was explained to my mother's minister who happened to be working away down in Fife at the time and he suggested marrying them there, in his parish. As

neither of them had any connections there, they felt perfectly
justified in having only Uncle Frank and Aunt Susie as best man
and bridesmaid at the church. The four of them then went to a
local restaurant to celebrate the occasion. Amongst my parents'
wedding presents, was a beautiful mahogany afternoon tea tray
with fine brass handles. My father's boss, the sub post master,
had personally made it for him and had very generously stuck
two five pound notes to it before presenting it to him – ten
pounds was a considerable amount of money in those days. On
their return to Orkney from their honeymoon, friends and family
were waiting at the 'Hope pier to welcome the happy couple
home and they had barely set foot on land before they were
whisked away to a surprise second reception at my
grandmother's house. When the time finally came to leave for
their new, more or less finished home, they were showered with
confetti and given a memorable send-off.

My parents, married in Fife in 1939.

After the war my father took the opportunity to make
several improvements to Hameneuk with salvaged materials
abandoned by the Services. He had learnt a considerable
number of skills during his wartime spell in the Royal Signals.
He started by connecting the house to what had previously been
the army's main water supply which conveniently ran along the
road outside. He then managed to salvage enough cable to wire up the whole house, and connect it
to the small diesel generator he had in his workshop to provide power and electric lighting. When
the neighbours saw Hameneuk "lit up" they were very impressed by my father's resourcefulness and
skill. As there was no mains electricity supply to the island in those days, to have both lighting and
power for an electric iron was quite a privilege. Spurred on by his domestic success he set up an
electric line to the school powered by the same generator. He then managed to salvage a further
quantity of cable which he laid along dykes and under roads in order to connect up six more
houses, virtually becoming the first local 'electricity board.' The hours of supply were originally set
by my father, but extra hours of electrical supply could be negotiated. He made a small charge for
the supply of power, calculated by adding the cost of the diesel fuel to any other expenses incurred
and dividing the total by the number of users. He received his supply free of charge in lieu of
payment for his services. However his job as a postman necessitated an early start and the requests
for additional supply meant waiting up late to turn the generator off, keeping him from his bed, so
he devised a clever timing device to turn the power off automatically. He used the mechanism from
an old alarm clock which had a
cotton reel fixed to the winding
stem. A length of strong
thread, with a small weight
attached to the end, was fixed
to the drum and wound round
it. The alarm was then set and
my father would go to bed.
When the alarm went off, the
cord unwound, pulling a pin
out of the generator throttle.
The engine would slowly

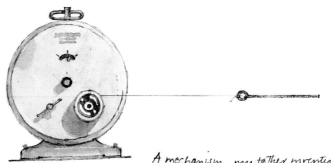

A mechanism, my father invented,
designed to switch off the Perkins diesel
engine which drove the generator.

shudder to a halt cutting the electrical supply off. It took a while to come to a complete stop, so the lights never went out immediately. There were always a few precious moments left to try to finish whatever you were doing. I can remember lying in bed at night, looking at a picture book when, at about eleven o'clock, the lights would gradually start to dim and I would make a frantic attempt to get to the end of the book before they finally went out.

My father built the workshop a couple of years after the war was over. He salvaged eight steel 'couples' (girders) and sheets of galvanised iron from disused Nissen huts and laboriously straightened them out to make the frame for the pitched roof of his garage. As they were all curved, he had to devise his own ingenious levering system to straighten them as far as possible. He then completed the job by hammering out any remaining curve on the garden wall. The boundary wall was built entirely with stones salvaged from a disused air raid shelter near the wartime naval base at the 'Hope pier. He thought it was wonderful to make something from nothing.

I spent the rest of the day walking and thinking about what my father had told me about my birth back in 1940. It wasn't straightforward and the regular island doctor, who apparently was very good, had left the practice just a few weeks before I was due and the lady doctor who attended to my mother, in his absence, was considered by my father not to be so good. It seems she hardly knew anything about my mother. There was only a district nurse on the island at that time, so she was in attendance at the birth even though she had very little obstetric experience. Through no fault of her own her training had been cut short by the onset of war. My father had called her out to Hameneuk in the morning to check that my mother was alright and that her pains signalled the onset of labour. When the nurse arrived, she confirmed that the early stages of labour were indeed underway and tried to make her as comfortable as she could. She then took herself off with her poetry book to settle down in the lounge for a good read as she saw little point in just sitting around in the 'delivery room' – there was nothing that she could do until the birth was imminent. The labour progressed very slowly and painfully and my father began to feel that things were not going as smoothly as they should. He repeatedly asked the nurse to let him through into the bedroom to be with his poor, suffering wife. She however, held very strong, textbook views on the presence of fathers-to-be in the delivery room, whether it was at home or not, and had no intention of conceding to my father's pleas – it was simply not done and that was that! Mothers-to-be should be left to 'get on with it' by themselves until the necessary midwifery skills were called for. My poor father was just left to his own devices which entailed pacing around the house, smoking cigarette after cigarette and downing a good bottle of port during the day (or maybe it was sherry, he wasn't sure) and waiting for the baby's first cry. As the seemingly interminable hours dragged by he could no longer bear either the strain of my mother's increasing cries or the apparent indifference of the nurse – he simply had to do something to help my mother. Almost at the end of his tether, he decided there and then to ring an army doctor who had made him an offer of help some while ago. He told my father that if he ever found himself facing an emergency, he was to call him immediately. Undoubtedly, childbirth fell into that category, so he quickly telephoned the army doctor and asked him if he would come right away to see to my mother who was obviously experiencing an increasingly difficult first labour with only a part trained, inexperienced nurse on hand. The doctor, sensing the urgency in my father's voice, gathered up the medical equipment and medicines he might need and arrived just in time to take charge of the situation. A forceps delivery of a big, healthy baby boy at the end of a complicated and exhausting forty-eight hour labour was necessary. To this day my father says he can still see the forceps boiling away sterilising, on top of the range in the big soup pot.

After the army doctor had safely delivered me, and put in the necessary stitches with characteristic precision (and with very little assistance from the inexperienced nurse), my father paid for his services with a half bottle of whisky and two hundred cigarettes! Immensely relieved that her

ordeal was over and now delighted with her new baby, my mother needed to regain her strength and health – she was completely drained. By contrast, I was fighting fit and ready for my first feed – and my poor mother would have to wait for her much needed rest! My father remembers the next few months well. Compensation for her suffering came in the enjoyment of watching the baby that had almost cost her her life, grow into a strong, noisy and determined little character.

I was a healthy, happy baby – only a few weeks later I was hit by meningitis.

CHAPTER 3

Silence Begins

The following morning, Bob, Maggie and I walked up to the general store which I remembered so well. It was one of the original shops in St Margaret's Hope. Before access to the Mainland, the main island in Orkney, became no more than a short drive across the Barrier roads, the village sustained a good range of shops. There were three bakers, a couple of butchers, two drapers, a chemist, an ironmongers, a Post Office, a boot shop, and several other grocers and at least one jewellers' shop. Sadly today, less than half of them remain. After the island was linked to the Mainland, the population began to disperse and local trade dwindled. Shops were forced to close and only a few, including the one we were about to visit, remained viable.

The entrance to the shop was through a new glass door. The interior had been completely rearranged, and the counters of long ago had been replaced with modern shelf-lined aisles brimming with goods. Tinned foods, elastic bands and pencils, fruit and veg, cereals and sugars, jams, sweets, stationery, pocket money priced items, dairy produce, bread, cakes, tights, ice cream, socks and patent remedies for minor ailments amongst a host of other items were stocked. We eased our way past the shoppers, through to the rear of the shop. I introduced myself to one of the assistants and asked if Jim Doull, the owner, was available and if so, would she please tell him that Hamish Rosie would like to see him. He soon came hurrying out and greeted me like a long lost

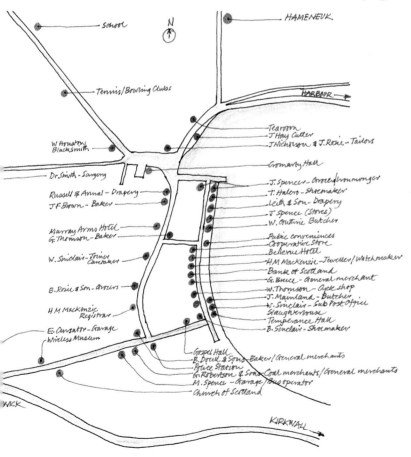

friend. I introduced my friends and when I explained that Maggie was going to record my story, he immediately offered to show us round the shop premises which, he explained, had expanded considerably since my time. In a store to the rear – an old bakery – Jim pointed out an old bread oven still intact and the bread paddles he had kept as a memento. I remembered it all from my childhood.

I had often come down to this very place to watch Benny, Jim's brother, at work. I loved the warmth and smell of the bakery. Watching him work the dough and shape it into loaves and scones with his floury hands was fascinating. I felt an affinity with this very quiet man and somehow we managed to communicate with each other – I can't remember how, but we did.

Benny prepared his dough in the usual way but in

When I was a small boy, I used to love visiting many shops in the village .....

15

order to get it to an even thickness, similar to that of a biscuit, he used an old mangle to 'roll' the dough through it! The yeast oven scones were then cut out and placed in a 'press' or steam cupboard to raise them before they were baked. This process gave them their special lightness. The steam, which I remember very well as a child, was very simply generated by heating an old iron farm implement up to a very high temperature and then throwing it into a bucket of cold water placed in the bottom of the cupboard. The resulting clouds of steam enveloped the scones.

We moved further into the store and Jim brought out a large wooden board covered with various odd brass knobs, switches and fittings. This, he explained, was an original, rather primitive but very effective circuit board made by my father. He had come across it when he took over the shop. The board had been used in the days when my father supplied electricity to the shop from his generator. It was used to control all the electrics in the shop:

We were then taken out to see the new mobile shop. It was a beautiful new Mercedes van, stocked and ready for the day's rounds – a far cry from the the old converted Bedford van that I remembered. The mobile shop was and still is an invaluable service to the more remote sections of the island community who depend on it for their regular supplies. Jim told us that years ago, in winter, he often would be out there in oilskins battling against the driving wind and rain, trying to measure out the paraffin for the old heaters people had in those days. But whatever the weather, the mobile shop went out.

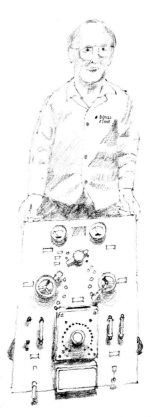

Jim Doull showed off the switch board, made by my father. His shop was supplied with electricity by my father. Jim still has the switch board as a reminder of old days.

As the Doulls had bought my parents' house when they left Orkney, Jim turned to me and suggested that we might like to go up to Hameneuk for a cup of coffee with his wife, Vera.

On our way up to Hameneuk, we passed the little sub Post Office on the Front Road where my father once worked. It was now converted into a house. Further along, I remembered the very spartan public toilet that used to be there. It was a small, stone hut that jutted out over the sea so that the waste went straight into the water. Mysteriously, torn up newspaper squares for use as toilet paper were sometimes supplied. Using the convenience was a very drafty operation and the waves often crashed dangerously around

Front Road, the sub post office, where my father worked with the slaughterhouse below can be seen on the left.

underneath. I only ever used it in a real emergency and then made sure I spent as little time as possible in there!

In the village there used to be a watchmaker-cum-chemist-cum-almost everything, as well as being the local registrar! Whenever I passed his shop, I would go in – his intricate work fascinated me. I would often find him bent over a watch or clock that he was repairing. He obviously knew how much I enjoyed watching him work and let me stay for hours at a time. On one occasion, he

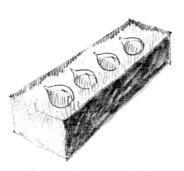

Small box containing stink bombs!

brought out a surprise present for me. When I opened the box I saw that it contained a number of small glass balls packed in sections, each with a small amount of liquid inside – genuine stink bombs! I was old enough and had been at school long enough to know exactly what they were. This was the best present anyone could have given me! We smiled knowingly at each other. I thanked him and wandering along the road outside, I saw the public convenience and noticed it was occupied. This would be an ideal opportunity. I carefully checked that no one else was in the vicinity, crept up to the hut and dropped one of the small glass balls just by the door. The glass shattered and I ran to where I knew I would be out of sight but could still see the toilet door, and waited. Almost immediately the door was thrust open and a very pinched faced and embarrassed occupant rushed out. A perfect result – I was delighted and happily no one ever found me out!

We passed the buildings that once housed the ironmongers' and general store – J. Spence and Son. I remembered one of the Spence brothers had a great love of nature and wildlife and bred blue tits up at his house. He developed such an affinity with them that they would sit on his hand and feed from it. I was allowed to watch. I thought it was magical, the birds seemed so delicate and tiny.

The road that runs past Hameneuk carries on over the hill, down to the farm where, as a child, I was sent by my mother to fetch the milk. I never liked going as it meant walking a mile each way along what was then a rough track so I always took my dog, Laddie, with me to keep me company. It seemed a very long way especially in the freezing winter weather but it was one household duty my mother insisted I did whether I liked it or not.

Our pet dog, a cairn terrier, Laddie.

Arriving at Hameneuk, I noticed with pride that the 'pavements' made with the slate from Swona were still there. Jim's wife, Vera, welcomed me at the door, with open arms and ushered us into the hall. After introducing my friends, I stood for a few moments, taking everything in, feeling peculiarly strange at being back in my childhood home after so many years. Vera said that Hameneuk was more or less the same as when I lived there and led us through into the kitchen to make coffee. The wonderful open view from the window out across the 'Hope transported me back years to my childhood.

When I was about three years old, I remember playing in the garden. My mother was working in the kitchen where she could keep an eye on me from the window. I had noticed a friendly looking animal in the field next door. He seemed to be looking at me so I thought I would go and stroke him. I managed to clamber over the dry stone wall into the field and started to walk towards him. My mother in the meantime had taken one of her frequent looks out of the window to check on my whereabouts, and saw to her horror that I was in the next field, calmly walking towards the local farmer's prize bull! She had to think very quickly as it was useless shouting to me – I wouldn't hear – she ran out of the house across to Smiddybank farm to get help. Fortunately she found the farmer at home. He dropped everything, tore up to the field with her, climbed over the wall and swiftly scooped me up out of harm's way. By that time, I was only a few feet away from the interesting animal with the ring in his nose, totally unafraid and utterly unaware of the danger! My poor mother – she had so much to cope with, and there was so much I would have to be taught.

Maggie, Bob and I sat down in the kitchen to coffee with Vera and after we had talked over old times she invited us to stay for lunch. It would be wonderful to be able to spend more time in my childhood home, I had so many memories. I was already thinking about the mischief I had got up to in this very kitchen when my mother was out of sight! I remember a lovely black cat that I had as a little boy. I loved to stroke and play with her. She felt soft and warm and although I couldn't hear her miaow, I could feel her purring. One day, quite unexpectedly, she produced four kittens. I loved to watch them playing, biting, pawing and crawling all over each other in the warmth and safety of the kitchen. They seemed to be having such fun that I innocently thought I would join in their rough and tumble. I was too young to know that I might endanger their lives by getting in amongst them and although I could see the mother cat looking anxiously at me with her mouth open, I couldn't hear her warning noises and so continued my 'wrestling' game with her kittens. Luckily my mother returned to the kitchen in time to extricate me from the litter and remove me from the protective mother cat before she lashed out. My mother tried very hard to make me understand that I was much bigger and heavier than them and might easily squash or hurt them, albeit unintentionally. But it was impossible to keep me away from them so she put them in a basket

Two of my four kittens at Hameneuke.

and took them and the mother cat over to Heads Farm where they would be right out of harm's way. This was the same farm that I was sent to every day to fetch the milk and not long after, as I approached the dairy, the mother cat walked out, took one look at me and momentarily froze with a look of distinct terror on her face. She must have recognised me because a split second later, she flew off to protect her litter from the unwelcome visitor. I then realised why my mother had taken the kittens to the farm.

No sooner had Vera set down some bowls of home-

Walking home from Heads where I collected milk, this view of St Margaret's Hope was memorable Hameneuke is just behind this big house on the left.

made broth and fresh bread on the kitchen table, than Jim walked in to join us. Over lunch, he reminded me of how he came to buy Hameneuk. When he knew my parents were going to move down to Aberdeen, he asked my father without delay if he would sell his house to him. Jim was very keen to buy it because he knew it was well built, in an excellent position and was generally a very desirable property. The sale was settled straight away and the house never went on the market. Jim and Vera moved in shortly after my parents left and have lived there ever since. After lunch Vera asked us if we would like to look round the rest of the house. I could not have hoped for more. She took us across the hall and opened a door into a bright, fresh bedroom. This, she told me, was where I first saw the light of day. My thoughts went to my poor mother, her difficult delivery, and the challenge I presented her with a few months later.

I learned about this 'challenge' from my father. He remembers me being a fairly vociferous baby with the usual vocabulary of sounds, noises and gurgles, cries and shouts. I have no memory of the sound of my own voice but I suppose I must have heard it as a baby. At ten months I spoke my first word "Mama," my father has a clear recollection of the event. Unfortunately, this little milestone in my life was to have a bitter twist for my parents. Shortly afterwards, I suddenly became critically ill but the newly returned doctor assured my mother that the symptoms, although appearing acute, indicated nothing more than a serious bout of teething trouble. The pressure which he felt was causing the extreme discomfort could be relieved by lancing my gum with just an ordinary, sterilised needle – which he did. My parents were, however, very uneasy with this diagnosis and treatment, but there was no hospital on the island to which they could take me for advice and, any hope of a second medical opinion lay at least an hour's boat journey away over on the Mainland. Neither parent could stand by, just seeing their baby's condition deteriorate, so

My father coming home after dropping the doctor at Hope Pier, worrying about my mysterious severe illness.

characteristically, my father took the law into his own hands. He telephoned the doctor in Kirkwall to explain their predicament and asked him if he would be prepared to come out to the island to give a much needed second opinion. To his immense relief, the doctor agreed and my father set off in a hired boat to bring him across to St Margaret's Hope. Within a few hours the doctor was up at Hameneuk carefully examining me. I was becoming increasingly distressed so he tested me for suspected meningitis, finding every symptom present with the exception of the tell-tale stiffness of the neck. He, too, eventually put the condition down to some acute form of childhood trouble, which he felt sure a strong and healthy baby like me would get over by himself, in due course. So despite my obvious suffering, no form of treatment was offered, no medicine prescribed, not even M&B (May & Baker) tablets – a patent medicine that was commonly prescribed to help with infections before penicillin was readily available. All that was left for my father to do, was to pay the doctor's fees and see him safely back on to the hired boat to the Mainland. As he walked back to Hameneuk he felt peculiarly helpless – it seemed unbelievable that absolutely nothing could be done to help his son, in his mind there had to be something that could be done. Not long after my father's return, I finally slipped into unconsciousness. Despite the apparent hopelessness of the situation, my mother refused to give up hope and bravely fought back the mounting despair she felt. She sat beside my cot for three long days keeping a faithful watch twenty-four hours a day, talking trustingly to my small, unnaturally silent and motionless form, positively willing me to show just a hint of response.

Eventually on the third day, fighting extreme tiredness, my mother saw me make a slight, but distinct movement towards her with my head as I slowly regained consciousness. Her sense of elation was indescribable. She ran to share the news with my father and they both openly wept tears of relief and exhaustion. All she wanted to do was to pick me up, hug me and hold me tightly to her but she felt she must restrain herself. I would be weak from my ordeal and lack of nourishment of any sort during the last seventy-two, dark hours. My father recalls how my mother then, very gently, took me in her arms, to give me "just a welcoming sip" of my favourite rhubarb juice from a teaspoon. She had prepared it convinced that I would survive. Later the illness was confirmed as having been meningitis.

My mother began to rediscover the enjoyment and rewards of her new motherhood, lavishing care and attention on me as I made a remarkably quick recovery. However, something about me began to trouble her deep down. She noticed that I seemed to need unusual coaxing into looking at her when she talked to me and, when she sang to me she saw my gaze absently wandering round the room from the safety of her arms. She would repeat my name again and again and yet, without attracting my attention by tickling my tummy, I did not instinctively respond. Sometimes in the past, when she put me in my cot to play, she would go out into the garden and play a game with me through the window but now she became aware that I was not immediately attracted by her knocking on the window. If I was looking away, I appeared to ignore her altogether. I no longer sat looking at the window, waiting for her face to pop up unexpectedly and surprise me, something that always made me laugh. She wondered if it was just possible that I was so deeply absorbed in my own thoughts and play that I simply could not be distracted – although she knocked on the window quite hard and repetitively? Gradually her innermost feelings began to tell her something that no mother, particularly a new one, would want to know – her baby was apparently not hearing things as he should. As the weeks and months went by, there also seemed, somehow, to be a lack in my general "advancement". Reluctantly my parents were forced to the cruel conclusion that their son's hearing had been paralysed by his illness. Although happy and otherwise fully recovered, I had become a virtual island unto myself at only ten months old.

This presented my mother with a formidable challenge. She had little knowledge of deafness, there was no specialist help on the island and the world was at war. But she had seen me pull through a life-threatening illness, without hospitalisation or medication and knew that this small miracle would become the foothold of my future. She was a resilient, self-disciplined and educated woman who took a long term view of the situation. She was determined to give me the best possible opportunity in life rather than just a chance of survival in the hearing world. Her vision for me inevitably involved having to face serious dilemmas, making extremely tough decisions and having to overcome constant hurdles. My mother's resolve became my starting point. She was keenly aware of what I had lost through my illness, I could laugh, cry and scream but would never know the sound of my own voice or her's. I would never hear the birds singing, or the sound of the sea or anything that she could hear. I had no memory of sound and was far too young to have acquired any language. Despite the seeming hopelessness of the situation, my mother knew she would, somehow, have to explore every possible way of teaching me how to communicate. Both my parents resolved that my first precious word should not become my last! But how and where to start – they themselves had little knowledge of deafness. These early days were often dark, difficult and deeply frustrating, but my mother's training and experience as a teacher helped her to come to terms and deal with the situation. Her own feelings had to be put aside in order to focus on giving me a basis for communication at a level that I could eventually grasp and use as I grew from a baby into a small boy. Fortunately she was level-headed, good-humoured, patient and, above all, persistent; qualities that were invaluable to her in meeting the challenge that she and my father faced.

She learned to attract my attention in various ways – rocking my cot, tapping me, turning my head to face her, or waving at me – it took endless patience. Right from the start my mother set a daily routine so that I came to learn and know the security of a sequence of regular events. Despite the apparent severity of my deafness she never gave up talking and singing to me normally, always making sure she looked directly at me so that I could see her face clearly and watch her lips making the shapes of the words. Patiently my mother went out of her way to point out things to me, showing me familiar things around the house, repeating their names to me over and over again making sure that I watched her lips as she did so. When she took me out she continued the same routine. She hoped and prayed that one day I might just learn to mimic one or two of them myself. It was important to encourage my visual awareness even though I would probably not understand very much. She and my father knew how important it was to stimulate me visually because unlike hearing babies I could not experience or respond to any form of sound and might easily not make any effort to come out of myself, if I was left to my own devices.

In time, I would have to learn how to use my eyes as my ears. My mother frequently picked me up and cuddled me. She instinctively felt that physical contact was very important for me. It communicated an immediate sense of security without words. So, apart from my progress being very slow, I had a fairly 'normal' babyhood and grew into an, otherwise, 'normal' mischievous toddler.

Vera closed the front bedroom door and as we walked across the hall to the sitting room, I was reminded of an amusing boyhood incident with a flour siever. My mother had been baking in the kitchen and I had been watching her and 'lending a helping hand,' when she was called away to the door. The baking still had to be finished, so she wiped her floury hands on her apron and told me to stay in the kitchen whilst she went to answer the door. She carefully shut the inner hall door to ensure that I stayed in the house, if not in the kitchen, and so as not to have to keep an eye on me. I had learned exactly what I was allowed and was not allowed to touch on baking days. But I soon became bored so scanned the kitchen for something with which

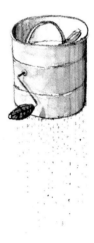

My mother's flour siever, I turned the handle to sieve the flour onto the floor!

to amuse myself. The flour siever on the table looked as though it might be fun. I had seen my mother use it and been fascinated by the flour showering down into the mixing bowl. I remembered she first filled it with flour, so I followed her example. I had also seen her turn the little handle on the side to sieve the flour through the fine mesh. So I did the same. To my delight, a small snow storm of soft, fine flour fell on to the kitchen floor. It looked so pretty that I decided to give the whole floor the same treatment! I walked round the kitchen turning the little handle, gradually carpeting it in virgin white. It was very satisfying and I decided to extend the job to the entire

21

ground floor of Hameneuk! I was doing a really thorough job, making sure that I went right into all the corners. Everywhere looked beautiful when I had finished. I was very pleased with myself. When my mother eventually opened the inner hall door, she was horrified and in no uncertain terms made me understand that she was going to tell my father when he came home. I knew this would be really awful, because he would be very cross with me. And he was. When he came home and heard what I had done, he picked me up and put me into a big, dry barrel outside, so that I would have to stay there and learn a lesson, with no chance of escape! Although I wasn't there for very long, it seemed like hours. Even though I was naturally quite mischievous, I usually knew the difference between having fun and being naughty. Just knowing that I was not to do something was not enough. I often had to find out why not for myself which sometimes led to trouble. My lack of language prevented any proper questioning or explanation. I needed to try things out. On very rare occasions my father had to use the threat of punishment as a deterrent if I was deliberately naughty or if there was likely to be a question of danger. Then there was never any question of misunderstanding on my part.

    Vera took us through into the sitting room and as soon as I saw the fireplace, another boyhood escapade came to mind. Materials were scarce during the war and so it was customary to 'mend and make do' and recycle everything possible. My mother, who loved to dress me up and take me out visiting, wanted me to have a new pair of velvet shorts for these occasions. She had an old blue velvet dress that she no longer used and thought the fabric might be used to make me some. When she told my father, he set to and made a pattern for them himself so the tailor would only have to make them up. That way he felt the tailor wouldn't charge quite so much. My mother was delighted with the end result and dressed me up to take me out to tea with her friends. She finished dressing me in my finery – the blue velvet shorts, a frilled, silk shirt, white socks and shiny black patent shoes, and then made sure I understood that I was to be a "good boy" and stay in the sitting room whilst she got herself ready. I have never been very patient and even as a very small boy, I did not like to be kept waiting! Sitting still in a big armchair, I looked around to see what I could do. Then I began to think about hiding myself. There were lots of places to hide in the sitting room and it would be fun to hide from my mother, but I would need to find somewhere that she wouldn't think of straight away. So I started to explore the obvious places – behind a chair, under the table, but I knew I would soon be discovered there. Then I looked at the fire place and wondered what went on inside the chimney breast. With innocent enthusiasm, I scrambled into the hearth to look up inside it. I could just see a small gap so I slowly eased my head up through it and then

Me, dressed in my best clothes – a moment before I explored up the chimney.

managed to squeeze the rest of my body up into the chimney cavity by levering myself up from a small inner ledge. It was very dark and sooty up there and there was nowhere to stand or sit. I hadn't thought about that but I was not going to be defeated now I had got this far – it was a wonderful hiding place. I decided to try to hold myself in place by pushing up with my arms from the little ledge. I desperately hoped that I was high enough up the chimney for my legs to be out of sight! It was quite a strain on my arms and I wasn't sure how long I would be able to hang on, but I was determined to stay there as long as possible – my mother would never find me there! When she returned to the empty sitting room and couldn't see me anywhere, she

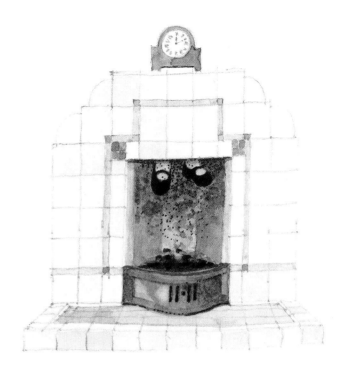

My mother was horrified to see my feet dangling in the fireplace.

became extremely worried. It was no use calling me because I wouldn't hear, so she started to search the room, looking for me in the most unlikely places knowing what an adventurer I could be. She had to find me. Meanwhile, up inside the chimney, I had no idea my mother had returned and was already looking for me. My little arms started to give way and very reluctantly I began to sink down from my hiding place unaware of the noise that I was making. My mother turned round to investigate the strange sounds coming from inside the chimney and saw a small, sooty but familiar pair of feet dangling in the fireplace. She could hardly believe what she saw! I felt her take hold of my feet and carefully ease me down to safety. I was black from head to toe! She was very cross with me but she was not going to let this spoil her afternoon. She quickly took off my sooty clothes and took me into the bathroom for a thorough wash. I was then dressed in my ordinary clothes and taken out to tea as planned by my baffled and disappointed mother. She had really been looking forward to showing me off in my new blue velvet shorts!

Maggie and I peeped into the bathroom where I noticed that the lock on the door was the original one. I remembered the mechanics of it very clearly. And the hatch in the ceiling leading up into the roof space was still there. That was where Christmas presents were hidden away until the big day. I can't remember how I discovered that fact, but once I had, I had to see it for myself. Every so often, I would go into the bathroom, shut the door, carefully open the hatch and sneak up the ladder to peep at the tantalising packages. I recounted the incident to my father recently. He had no idea and was amazed at my daring and that I had never fallen from the ladder. Apparently neither he nor my mother had any idea about my secret Christmas previews which really surprised me! More often than not, the unusual noises my escapades evidently made, gave me away. I, of course, had no idea how I could be so easily detected until I learned that most actions and movements had associated 'sounds'. Although my previews gave me quite a thrill, deep down, I actually felt rather guilty. I knew it was wrong. My parents would have been very disappointed at having their well kept Christmas secrets spoilt.

Before leaving, Vera took us out to see the small wash house at the back of Hameneuk that my father built. Inside she showed us the same stone sinks with which he had replaced the original wooden tubs. They had survived years of wear and tear. I thought back to laundry days with my mother, watching her busily rubbing and scrubbing away on her washboard in the sink, giving special attention to collars and cuffs with a big bar of household soap. Everything was rinsed clean and then put through the mangle. It had long since disappeared but I remember feeling very important at being allowed to turn the handle for her. I used to really enjoy seeing the bulky, wet washing squeezing through the rollers being transformed into long, thin, flat shapes. As soon as my mother had finished the laundry, I would quickly run outside to watch the water from the sinks empty out along a little gully cut into the slate 'pavement', down into the drain.

Reluctantly, we said our goodbyes to Vera and thanked her for her hospitality and for showing us round Hameneuk. It had been a very special time for me and had enabled my friends to see the home that I had told them so much about.

Top floor of the house on the left where my blue velvet shorts were tailored.

CHAPTER 4

Facing Reality

I thought a great deal about my mother over the next few days and of how she had selflessly taken the long term view of my situation. Being a qualified teacher she knew that education would be the key to the hearing world. At that time the vocational opportunities for those not fortunate enough to receive an early education were few and virtually non-existent for a deaf person. She knew that I would need to start my education at the earliest opportunity. But to enable me to benefit from any education, conventional or specialist, I would first need to acquire some language and learn how to communicate. My parents discussed what might be done for me and my father felt that, with her training and experience, my mother would be best suited to making initial enquiries about any schooling opportunity there might be. They both knew that their family situation would only be short term, for as the war progressed, my father's call-up papers could come through any day. He tried to put this very real possibility to the back of his mind as the idea of my mother being left completely alone to bring me up and find a way of educating me was a matter of great concern to him. Even with my father at home, it would not be the easiest task for my mother to undertake – there was a war on, communication and travelling restrictions were imposed and we lived away up in Orkney.

In the early summer of 1943 when I was three years old, my father's call-up papers eventually arrived. Although both my parents had privately anticipated their arrival for some time, it still came as quite a shock when it happened. His going away on active service meant that my mother would now have to take total responsibility for my future. She would have to find a way forward and search out a specialist education for me entirely alone and my father might never know what would become of me. I remained blissfully unaware of the fact that I was to be parted from him indefinitely. Recently, I learnt from my father that there was a possibility that he could have been exempted from military service through the intervention of the parish minister. He would have had considerable influence with the authorities. In those days a minister's word went a very long way. However as more and more men were needed, my father made a conscious decision not to avoid the call up even though it would have considerably relieved the burden on my mother. He knew he had a duty to King and Country.

On joining up my father first had to present himself for the statutory medical examination. He was passed as fit and able-bodied and was sent for an initial six week 'square-bashing' in Wales before he was sent to Boscombe to complete his training. Despite having to go to Wales, he did however manage to get 'harvest leave' which meant that he came back to the island for six weeks to work on a farm and was able to live at home with us. My mother was very grateful but as soon as the harvest was over, my father had to return to the south to join the Royal Signals for further training until he was posted.

News of his posting arrived several months later and he came home on a few days embarkation leave. I wasn't aware of the serious reason for his unexpected reappearance. I was just innocently pleased to have my 'Daddy' home once again. When the day for my father to leave for his posting abroad finally came,

My father, Private John T Rosie, active in Burma during the World War Two.

25

he and my mother decided to say their final farewells at Hameneuk rather then on the quayside in Kirkwall. They had previously discussed their impending parting and had decided that it should be kept as low key and simple as possible. My mother and I would not go to Kirkwall to see him off even though I might have better understood that my father had 'gone' if I had actually seen him board the ship and sail away. He felt that it would have been unnecessarily hard for my mother. We waved him off on his journey which eventually took him to Burma, where he spent the better part of his active service.

"Where is Daddy?" I tried to ask my mother time and time again after my father had left Hameneuk. I had no idea why he was suddenly not around any more. She knew exactly what I wanted to know and was at pains to try to find a way of helping me to understand that he had gone away to war. But the concept of war would be difficult enough for a hearing three-year-old to grasp, let alone a deaf one. All I can remember about the war was seeing 'flashes' on the ground and the searchlights reaching up into the night but at that time I didn't understand their significance. Hameneuk was very close to Scapa Flow, one of the prime targets of the Second World War. There was plenty of action to be seen in the air and out to sea, my father recalls from the time before he was called up. There were lots and lots of raids – especially around Scapa Flow, even though it was said that some of the enemy aircraft would sometimes divert out to sea to drop their bombs in the water rather than on the islands.

Day after day, week after week, I followed my mother round asking her over and over again where 'my Daddy' was, and could never understand her answers. I was totally bewildered. I missed my father's presence greatly and was very perplexed about where he was – why had he said goodbye one morning and not come home as he usually did in the afternoon. But I was unable to work out an answer for myself. I had to slowly grow used to the fact that my father had just mysteriously disappeared and get used to life alone with my mother. Looking back, these early years with my mother strengthened and deepened the bond between us.

Throughout the war my mother wrote at least once a week to my father, and she made sure he was kept abreast of her plans for my education. Each of her letters was numbered so that my father would know whether all or only some of his post was getting through. The envelopes were simply addressed to Private John T. Rosie, with no address or destination. My father recalled that it was really wonderful to get her letters and how it made him feel so good. He made every attempt to write to her once a fortnight but as the content of all outgoing mail, including personal letters, was severely limited by censorship it was more a matter of just being able to keep in touch with her than being able to send home any real news. My mother was always so relieved to hear from him despite the formal content of his letters. He also sent her anything he was able to save out of his ten shillings a week army pay. As he says, he was "looked after – fed and clothed," so he had little need of money.

My mother had been left with the responsibility of my upbringing. Despite the difficulties and deprivations of wartime life, she kept my long term future uppermost in her mind as she tackled the lonely and daunting task of investigating the way in which I could be educated. As there were no specialist facilities or advice whatsoever on the island, my mother knew that before long I would have to leave the warmth and security of my island home if there was to be any hope of the sort of education that she wanted for me. It would necessitate me having to leave home to board somewhere. Any expertise had to be brought across from the Scottish mainland. Her first task was to get a hearing specialist to come to Orkney to assess my deafness. After much effort, she did so successfully. He confirmed the severity of the situation. I seemed to have no hearing at all and that there was very little that could be done for me – hearing aids were unavailable for children at that time. The best that my mother could hope for my future, was for me to eventually learn some manual skill so that I could become either a joiner or a mason and make a living from a trade. My mother however told him that she was not prepared to simply accept his prognostication yet. I was a bright and alert little boy despite my deafness. She wanted the best possible opportunity for me but needed advice on education for deaf children. The specialist was rather surprised at her reaction but suggested the only suitable educational institute he knew of, lay far away across the water in Aberdeen. My mother knew her vision for me would involve her having to accept many sacrifices, but at the same time she felt the first hint of encouragement about my future since I had lost my hearing. Although she would have to send me away to school, she knew it was the best possible thing she could do for me and had my father been there she would have had his full support. My mother and I left the visiting specialist, I blissfully unaware of what lay ahead.

Over the next few months, she liaised extensively with the school in Aberdeen, keen to learn about their teaching methods and the curriculum content. She wrote to tell my father of her findings and how pleased she was at having found some prospect for my future but how torn she was between giving me over to the school to get me an early start and desperately wanting to keep me with her. The longer I stayed 'isolated' at home the more difficult communication and interacting with other people would become and the harder the learning process would be. She alone took the decision to give me the best chance possible even though it involved sending me away to school. She applied to the special school in Aberdeen for a place for me to start at the beginning of the new academic year and then wrote to my father to tell him of her decision. At the young age of four I would have to board and would only return to my island for short, end of term holiday periods. Perhaps it was best that I had no idea of what was going to happen.

In the intervening period, my mother put thoughts of our forthcoming separation to the back of her mind determined to enjoy every minute of having me at home with her. At the same time she worked very hard to give me the start of a communication basis for the years ahead. "Watch my lips," she always said when she spoke to me. She painstakingly taught me to understand a very few basic words so that we would have a small way of communicating with each other by letter when I was away at school. Motivated by having found a specialist education for me and with great patience, she began to chip away at the invisible, silent barrier that threatened to isolate me from my parents and the world. It was extremely hard work. Besides learning to understand a few words, I developed keen powers of observation – essential to my development. I would have to learn to use my eyes instead of ears.

Even for a little boy, life without language was not easy. I liked to day dream and would want to share my ideas with my mother – but without any language it was almost impossible. So I would sit and bang my head endlessly against the wall out of deep frustration not knowing how to get through the intangible barrier of my silence. I knew my thoughts were normal because I knew them clearly, but why couldn't I make my mother or anyone else understand them? I had only the few words my mother had taught me and could only really communicate with facial expressions and gestures. But I was quite stubborn and rarely gave up. I often struggled on in a fury of temper and frustration determined to 'say' what I wanted to. My mother too suffered deep frustration when she was unable to get through to me, particularly when she had to make me understand things for my own safety. It was essential to make me grasp that certain things were wrong and could endanger me but it was extremely difficult in those early days.

In time she learned to interpret my 'tantrums' and emotional explosions as expressions of my natural ability to think and my deep need to find a way of communicating my thoughts. She came to my rescue and gradually helped me to learn how to enjoy periods of contented, uninterrupted play at Hameneuk.

CHAPTER 5 *School and Exile*

The long daylight hours of summer slowly gave way to the start of the school year. Finally, one day, my mother and I set off from Hameneuk for what I discovered was to be my school in Aberdeen. My mother had rented a room there in a doctor's house nearby so that I could start at the Aberdeen Special School for the Deaf as a day boy at the beginning of the year until a boarding vacancy occurred. Starting school and being with so many other deaf boys and girls was a new experience for me, but I adapted to it quite quickly and didn't mind going to school despite the teachers being very strict. I knew my mother would always be there to collect me so I could get through the day. I had no idea that before long I would become a boarder even though she had tried to explain this to me. She had also tried really hard to explain that I wouldn't be staying at school forever, I would go home to my island and Hameneuk in the holidays. These were impossible concepts to grasp at four years old without any real language. I felt safe with my mother and I loved my home in St Margaret's Hope, why would she want to leave me at school alone? I could not understand. The day came when she took me to school in the usual way waved goodbye to me but gave me an extra big hug and kiss. I turned round just as I went inside the building to see her still standing there waving – that was different

Aberdeen Special School for the Deaf, Polmuir Road, it was constructed with huge blocks of granite, where I spent ten years in my life.

from her normal routine. Things carried on as usual throughout the day but at the close of school lessons, instead of being allowed to leave the building with the other day pupils to meet my mother and go home, I found myself being shepherded with all the other deaf children into the boarders' spartan dining room for a communal high tea. The girls and boys sat separately. I remember that fateful first evening so well. It all felt so strange and I could barely eat my food. Then I followed the youngest boys and girls on their way up to their respective dormitories. I cried and cried all the way. I just couldn't stop myself. It felt as though my whole world had come to an end. Where was my mother? Had she forgotten me?

The boys were ushered into the bathroom once the girls had finished. The functional row of wash basins and two open baths were in stark contrast to the bathroom at home and I sobbed all the more as I dutifully washed my face and brushed my teeth. The other boys tried to comfort me.

They probably knew how I was feeling because they had started boarding at the beginning of the school year, but I was inconsolable. I wondered if I would ever see my mother again or perhaps she would just disappear like my father? It took me a very long time to settle in and I missed my own little room at Hameneuk and the luxury of sleeping in a big, comfortable double bed all of my own. Sleeping in a dormitory with lots of other boys felt very peculiar. From my first night on, I frequently cried myself to sleep under the bed clothes after the lights were turned out and no one could see me. My father had gone and it now seemed that I had been left at school forever by my mother. I really missed her. Eventually I had to get used to facing each day at boarding school and get on with the arduous business of acquiring language and learning how to communicate.

At school, any form of signing was frowned upon and strictly forbidden. This was supposed to ensure that all the children learned to develop oral communication and would be able to lip read. Anyone caught signing was punished with a smart whack across the knuckles from the edge of a ruler. So clandestine signing and simple gesturing were reserved for the dormitory at night. I never learned any form of recognised sign language before going to school as my mother was unaware of its existence and although I did use some gestures for communication, my 'first' language was really spoken rather than signed.

The boarders' school routine at that time verged on the military. The daily and weekly timetable continued throughout each term, it never varied – I knew precisely what to expect every day. Every morning we were woken at 6.45 sharp and after washing and dressing we all had to clean the classrooms. This work had to be completed before breakfast. Over the years my daily responsibility became sweeping the biggest classroom of all. On top of these regular duties, every so often, we were given additional tasks. Mine was to wax and polish the oak window frames, doors and wall panelling. On Saturdays yet another pre-breakfast job fell to us – cleaning the school toilets. After the chores were completed, we had to line up for our daily dose of cod liver oil, administered to each of us by the matron. I dreaded this – the taste was indescribably horrible, but there was no escaping it. Somehow my mother knew about this particularly grim necessity and how much I hated having the dreaded spoonful thrust into my mouth. So she hunted around to find some alternative for me and came across some delicious cod liver oil cream made by Thomson's of Elgin. She made arrangements for some to be sent to the school so that I wouldn't have to put up with the other awful preparation! My fellow boarders were very curious about why I started to be given something different from them. My mother knew how much I disliked the deprivation and rigours of boarding school and would often send me little treats like this to soften the experience.

Just before eight o'clock we would sit down, ten to a table in the dining room, to bowls of porridge. But it was no ordinary porridge. The matron herself made it every day. Somehow she never managed to achieve any semblance of a proper texture – it always consisted of a mass of huge lumps. My bowlful was often little more than a single solid lump – which I was made to eat. I tried and tried again to swallow it. It was really awful and made me feel sick, but eventually, with extreme difficulty, I managed it. After the 'porridge' came slices of white bread thinly spread with margarine but never any jam or marmalade with it. Food was scarce in those days, as we were constantly reminded. The older children probably understood that this was due to the war, but we little ones just had to accept what we were given. Breakfast finished with a cup of weak, milky tea poured ready mixed from a large aluminium teapot.

We then had to wash and dry the breakfast dishes. Domestic help was hard to come by during the war and so the school had only one such employee. She was a very large lady with a hard and rough manner towards all the boarders. Fortunately for us she only came in on a daily basis during the week which meant that we had some respite during the weekend. We took the various tasks of dish washing in turn. When it was my turn to wash up the enormous, heavy steel porridge pan, I remember scraping and scraping away at the thick coagulated layer in an attempt to loosen it and get down to the bottom to give it a good scouring. This was one of the worst jobs I ever had to do.

Once the daily chores were done, breakfast over, the dishes done and put away, the day pupils began to arrive and school lessons occupied the morning until lunch time. Every day was spent in the same classroom. Lessons always took the same form, the content seemed to vary very little and the iron rule of not being allowed to attend to any of nature's calls during the school day was never relaxed. This resulted in a number of accidents in the early days and some very uncomfortable 'wet' lessons.

In my ability to communicate, I was a couple of years behind my peers right from the start. With practically no language at all, work in the classroom was a mountainous struggle. In the early days, I understood practically nothing. It was a miserable time. We were taught English, geography, history and arithmetic. I just sat there watching what went on and observing the marks the teacher made as she wrote on the blackboard. It took years of constant repetition for me to very slowly begin to pick up a few things. Several times a week the speech therapist would come to our classroom to teach each of us how to use and understand our voices. She worked with very simple 'tools' – a balloon, a feather, a ruler and a spoon. I remember having my tongue pushed down with the spoon in an effort to teach me how to shape and speak individual letters. To make sure that I learned to pronounce sounds like 'e'

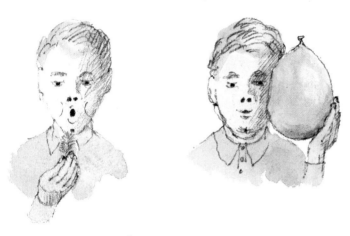

Speech therapy.

correctly, she used the ruler to keep my mouth in the necessary flattened position. Working with the balloon was much more comfortable. I held it with my hands whilst the speech therapist 'spoke' on to it so that I could feel the vibrations of the different sounds and words. Sometimes she would make me put the back of one of my hands on my throat and the other on hers whilst she spoke sounds like 'k', 'g' and 'x'. Then I had to try to recreate the vibrations myself by repeating them until I could feel mine matching hers. Learning to pronounce and differentiate between small soft sounds like 'p', 'b', 'v', 's' and 'z', was very difficult. I had to repeatedly pronounce 'puh' and 'buh' at a small feather. The slight difference in the movement of the feather helped me to identify, understand and learn the minimal difference. The most difficult sound to learn was the rolled Scottish 'r'. Learning to speak was a very long, arduous and demanding task but any lapse in concentration or effort resulted in punishment. It seemed particularly hard at the time. However, it did mean that I always tried my best. Although I could not understand the reason for the discipline at the time, the speech therapist knew that without it, my ability to communicate would not develop and any long term opportunities would be severely restricted.

At the end of the morning lessons, day pupils and boarders sat down to lunch together in the lunch time dining room. This was a much better affair in every way than either breakfast or high tea. It was served in an outbuilding which had been converted from its previous use as an enormous garage. It was kept spotlessly clean and tidy. The food was brought in by an outside catering firm and was far superior to any in-house cooking. This ensured that we boarders got at least one good meal a day during the week and at weekends lunches were prepared by a professional cook who came in to the school. Lunches were something to which all the boarders looked forward.

School lessons filled the afternoons. We were taught basic language and how to read and write very simple words and text. It all took me a very long time. Twice during the school week we were given letter writing lessons. The teacher would start a 'standard' letter on the blackboard and we would copy it down. After the usual 'I am well, etc' she would encourage us to add snippets of personal news to add to our 'standard' letters. I took a long time to reach this level as I was a very slow learner. I was lucky that my mother had had the foresight to teach me a very few basic words – 'Mummy', 'Daddy', my name and so on before I went away to school so at least I had something I could write. She was a great letter writer and wrote to me at least once a week. They were very simple letters using only the words I knew so that I would be able to understand what she wrote and they allayed my fears that she had disappeared entirely. She knew exactly what I needed to 'hear' – I treasured her letters. They helped me to escape from the cold, daily rigour of my school, back to the warmth of Hameneuk and at least I knew where my mother was. I could picture my home and my island and, at night, I would often wander around them in my mind before going to sleep.

Acquiring language was a truly mammoth task which I did not enjoy at all, but I loved to draw and paint, and from time to time we were allowed to do this. My mother encouraged me to draw almost as soon as I could hold a crayon. She would sit with me and draw pictures and 'show' me the names for each of the things that she drew in an attempt to help me learn them, but progress was extremely slow. I just enjoyed watching the pictures appear, but the words she drew were strange linear patterns that meant nothing to me. As I grew older I would lie for hours on the floor drawing and painting on lengths of old wallpaper. There was little money to buy drawing paper in those days but old wallpaper had its compensation – it provided me with a really large area to work in. Somehow I found I could 'talk' through colour, line, shape and form and convey a little of my feelings. These were elements that I began to find I could control, understand and use – unlike written or verbal language which was so difficult. Each word had to be individually learned and understood before I could use it with any hope of success. It was an excruciatingly slow process for me. My mother who drew quite a lot herself, recognised what seemed to be my natural feel for drawing and visual imagery very early on and helped me to develop this ability in support of my minimal language. She felt that drawing and painting could become a valuable area of development for me.

It seemed that at school, I began to show great promise in drawing and painting, even my classmates were impressed with my artistic attempts. I was fortunate that my teachers recognised my growing ability in this field and actively supported me. I was often encouraged to include a drawing with my twice weekly letters home. My mother really enjoyed receiving my art work, they almost meant more to her than my letters because she knew I had done them entirely by myself – I had chosen the subject matter (and it was often Hameneuk), decided on the composition of the picture and which colours to use. She was particularly moved by a very simple painting of a sailing boat sitting on the water in St Margaret's Hope harbour which I folded up neatly and sent home when I was about seven years old. The school never provided any art materials – not even paper. With the exception of letter writing lessons, when I could use note paper to draw and paint on, the best I could do was to unroll a length of toilet paper and use that. When my mother received my letter and its contents, she carefully unfolded the painting and was very impressed by my efforts. She really felt it was good enough to enter for a national children's art competition. However, the competition regulations stipulated that entries had to be submitted in flat form and my painting had been thoroughly creased, folded and sent through the post. But my mother had no intention of letting this stop her entering my work, so she carefully ironed out the folds and sent the painting off. Some weeks later, much to my amazement, I was told by the school that some of my work had won a commendation in a children's art competition and I was to be sent a prize for my efforts. My mother proudly represented me at a small exhibition of the competition work in Kirkwall as it took place during the term time and I was still away at school in Aberdeen. One of the judges – Stanley Cursiter RSA, a fellow Orcadian, introduced himself to her and made a point of telling my mother that, in his opinion, her son looked as though he could have considerable potential as an artist. She took his remarks very much to heart and became determined to encourage me to develop my talent at every opportunity. A huge brown parcel addressed to me arrived during the next school holidays – it was my prize. I could hardly believe it was really for me. I tore the paper off in great excitement to find a very generous range of real artist's materials, everything that I could ever have wished for – 'proper' paints and brushes, crayons and pencils, sheets and rolls of proper paper and a whole range of other useful materials. I was absolutely thrilled – this was the first time I had ever had any 'proper' materials. They proved to be a real inspiration to my work and helped me build up confidence in exploring what I could do with them.

When lessons were over and the day pupils had gone home, whatever the weather, we boarders were marched to the nearby park where for a wonderful hour or so, we were allowed to play or organise games of football or rounders ourselves without any involvement of the teacher. We weren't allowed to use real footballs in the school playground but had to make do with the giant woolly pompom balls that we made in the classroom. The games in the park were a very special time for each of us as it was the only occasion during the entire day when we were left to our own devices. Every minute of every other hour we were either having lessons or were under strict supervision. I remember once ignoring the school rule about footballs in the playground and playing with a real one. In a moment of enthusiastic play I accidentally smashed one of the toilet windows with it. I was terrified at the thought of being summoned to the headmistress' study for the transgression and resulting damage, but I knew I inevitably would be. As I walked in, her face was purple with rage

My toymaking, smashed from my laundry box. I was not supposed to do that but I did it twice so my father had to make two more boxes.

33

and she gave me a smart 'caning' on the hand with the thin edge of a ruler. It hurt a lot but I never, ever broke that school rule again.

Once this hour of precious freedom was over, we were marched back to school for the last meal of the day – high tea. It always seemed very dull and uninteresting after the catering firm's lunches. Servings were small and consisted of dried scrambled eggs, baked beans or something similar followed by bread and margarine and the ubiquitous cup of ready mixed weak, milky tea. Although we were fed what I expect was a reasonably balanced diet, I remember still feeling hungry at the end of the meals.

On Sundays the matron marched us a mile to morning service at a special church for the deaf. It had been converted from a large town house and had a social club for the deaf attached to it. The club provided a much needed opportunity for deaf people in the area to meet socially and communicate freely amongst themselves, away from the hearing world. Being dedicated to deaf people everyone signed and there was no oral communication. As regular church attenders, we were invited to the Christmas and Easter parties at the club. After the spartan régime of the Special School, these were very special events. That same club later became the focus of my social life. I always met up with my deaf friends there. Church services were the one recognised break from oral communication we had during the week – the entire service was signed by the minister. We sat in the front pews, reserved for children, to give us the best possible chance of following the service. Despite the abstract religious concepts he talked about being very difficult to grasp and understand, it was wonderful to be 'spoken to' in a visual language that we could follow with relative ease. There was, however, a price to pay. Deaf people were held in very low esteem at that time, and the local hearing youths took immense delight in hurling abuse at us as we walked to church. These local lads had even managed to find out how to sign, "Go to hell," to ensure we knew exactly what they thought of us. We were made to feel like outcasts. They knew retaliation was out of the question. Our only defence was to ignore them however hard it was.

After high tea, each boarder was assigned one or two further household duties. At just seven or eight years old, I was responsible for looking after twenty pairs of shoes – all the boarders' shoes. It was my duty to carefully inspect the soles and heels of each shoe, to check for wear and tear. If either were worn, I had to repair them by nailing either steel tips on to the heel or studs into the soles. After completing the necessary repairs, all the shoes had to be polished with either black or brown polish, until they shone. My work was then checked by the matron. She was a perfectionist and if there was any minute aspect of my work that fell below her high standards, I had to do it all over again until it met with her approval. Then each pair of cleaned and mended shoes had to be returned to the shoe store and placed in the appropriate owner's labelled box.

I had yet another weekly task to do, but it was one that I quite enjoyed doing as it reminded me of home. My mother had asked that I be allowed to send all my laundry home for her to wash and iron

Looking after twenty pairs of boarders' shoes – polishing and mending.

on a weekly basis. This helped her to play an active part in looking after me even though I was hundreds of miles away. My father made me a small, wooden box in which to send my weekly laundry home and every week the matron would help me pack my washing into it ready to send off. I remember it had a sliding lid with my home address on one side and my school address on the other so that it could be reversed to show the appropriate destination. I became very attached to this little household item because it gave me a tangible link with home during the long term time. I knew exactly where the box would be delivered at home and where and how my mother would untie the string, open and unpack it. I would almost be able to feel her saying that she "can't imagine how Hamish can get his clothes quite so dirty" and then I would imagine her taking them all out to the wash house at Hameneuk to give them a thoroughly good wash. She would then rinse them in the stone sinks before putting them through the

mangle to squeeze them almost dry. I knew the pattern so well. She would then take my clothes out into the garden and peg them out really securely to dry in the strong, South Ronaldsay wind. Looking contentedly at her son's little clothes flapping wildly on the line, my mother would enjoy the normality of a family wash day even though her 'family' was across the sea. Somehow it helped to bring her mentally close to me. When my clothes were dry she would take them in, heat up the flat irons on the range, iron them to perfection and neatly fold them to fit my little wooden laundry box after they had been properly aired. She would pack them, slipping in a Crunchie bar or two between the layers. She knew only too well the delight these little home treats would bring to me as I came across them unpacking my laundry in Aberdeen.

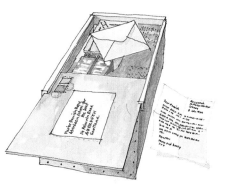

My laundry box, sent home every week. I looked forward to my mother's letter that accompanied my clean clothes.

The freshly laundered clothes that my mother always returned within the week brought the familiar feel and smell of my home back to me. As I opened my little laundry box I could picture my father at his workbench in his workshop at Hameneuk, where he had made the box. It made many weekly trips via the Royal Mail to and from South Ronaldsay before, driven by the lack of toys at school and a desire to demonstrate my inventiveness to my contemporaries, I rashly decided to reduce most of it to matchwood. I then used the pieces to make toy boats and planes and converted the remainder into a garage for my Dinky car. Although my classmates were suitably in awe of both my imagination and dexterity, my father was rather less so, particularly as he had to make a replacement box.

When all our household duties were satisfactorily completed, it was time for bed. Bedtimes ranged from five o'clock for the youngest pupils to nine o'clock for the sixteen year olds. There were four dormitories – two for the girls and two for the boys, irrespective of age differences. When I first started at the school, I was one of the youngest so went up to bed with my peers at five o'clock. We had to get undressed, wash, put our pyjamas on and then get into bed and lie there until the oldest boys came up four hours later. During that time, when the matron was out of sight we would enjoy 'signing' to each other with our homemade gestures. It was wonderful to be able to unwind and communicate with each other in our own way, away from the demands and pressures of oral communication. Once the sixteen year olds were in bed, the matron locked the dormitory doors for the night. The matron's room was located between the boys' and girls' dormitories, so she was on hand to unlock the doors if the need arose during the night but, looking back, it did seem an extraordinary thing to do. The older boys took a cruel delight in playing on the naïveté of the youngest boys by pretending to be ghosts and terrifying us. I had never experienced anything like it before and was absolutely convinced ghosts were real. I often hid under my blanket and spent the whole night there desperate to avoid their taunting and teasing – they could be very unkind.

As we were locked in the dormitory at night and could not get out to use the toilet, a zinc 'tub' was placed in the middle of the floor of the boys' dormitory for emergency purposes during the night. During the war years, the blackout blinds were pulled down so it was almost impossible to see where the improvised toilet was. I can remember crawling across the floor in the dark at five years old, feeling for the 'tub'. I didn't always manage to find it in the dark and often 'missed the target'. The older boys were responsible for emptying the 'tub' in the morning and would freely vent their wrath on any one who they suspected had not managed to aim straight in the darkness of the night.

This was my dormitory at Aberdeen school, it was locked all night and an oval galvanised steel tub was placed on the floor used as a toilet. No lights so we had to crawl to feel where it was.

One of my friends, Billy Allardyce, who slept in the bed opposite me, confided in me that he planned to run away from school. He had had enough of the tyranny. Nobody apart from me knew and I was sworn to secrecy. I thought he was very brave and daring. That night I forced myself to stay awake long after everyone else had gone to sleep. My eyes became used to the dark and I could see lots of movement going on under the bedclothes in the opposite bed – I knew exactly what was going on. Part of his escape plan was to get dressed without being seen, he even had to put on his shoes under the blankets and this seemed very exciting to me. The key point was not to be seen – any noise he might make would not wake anyone in the dormitory. I lay there feeling very honoured at being party to his plans, watching him carefully put his pillow into his bed and pull the blankets up over it which, he told me, would prevent anyone discovering that he was missing until the morning, by which time he would be safely at home. Billy then crawled across the floor, to avoid being seen, past my bed, waving a surreptitious goodbye to me. How he ever managed to unlock the dormitory door, I will never know! He crept down the stairs to the matron's office where the boarders' pocket money was kept in separately labelled tins, found his own and removed the contents as he needed the bus fare home. The entrance door was the only remaining barrier between Billy and freedom and luckily the key was in the lock. He carefully turned it and was out in the dark street and running to the bus stop before anyone saw him. In a very short time he was on the bus heading for home feeling very pleased with himself. Back at school I must have fallen asleep whilst trying to imagine what Billy would be doing and if he had managed to escape undetected. I wish I had been brave enough to escape but there would have been little point – my home was on an island, far away. He was lucky to live only a bus ride away. In the middle of the night, the dormitory lights suddenly went on and I awoke with quite a start to see Billy, looking very downcast, being marched in by an extremely angry and red-faced matron. She stood glowering over him while he got undressed and into bed, shot us all a warning look and told Billy she would see him in the morning. With that, she switched off the lights and locked us in for the rest of the night. Poor Billy, I didn't envy him now but I was very curious to know what had happened to him, how had he been caught, what could have gone wrong with his seemingly flawless plan? In the morning he told me that halfway home on the bus to Stonehaven, it unexpectedly stopped. He had no idea why and was astonished and confused to find himself suddenly escorted off the bus by two, plain-clothes policemen, into a waiting car. How could they have possibly known where he was? The worst thing that had happened to him was being inexplicably blindfolded by one of the policemen before he was driven back to school – possibly as a deterrent, so that he wouldn't see which way he was driven back. But suddenly not being able to see was terrifying for a young deaf boy. Like all deaf people, he relied on his eyes in place of his ears and, with neither, he became frighteningly disorientated.

As well as finding it very difficult to settle down as a boarder, I had a very bad experience during my first year at school. I began to feel very ill and developed a permanent stomach-ache. I started being violently sick and became badly constipated. The matron was well aware that something was wrong with me, but seemed to have failed to notice or perhaps 'believe' the symptoms I was manifesting despite seeing me doubled up with pain. Eventually she told me that I needed to rest and put me to bed in the dormitory. In those days there was no separate sickroom so if anyone contracted an infectious disease they were sent to an isolation room in the local hospital for the duration. I remember spending a lonely spell there myself when I had measles. I tried very hard to lie still in bed but I was in real agony and when I had to get out of bed to go to the toilet, I could only just manage to crawl across the floor. Luckily one of the older girls in the school, became aware of my state and the seriousness of the situation but it was very difficult for her to know what to do since we were ruled with a rod of iron, under constant supervision and daren't step out of line. She couldn't possibly question the matron's rest cure for me but if she was brave enough she could follow her instinct and get help for me. I don't know why, but she seemed to feel a genuine responsibility towards me, perhaps it was her maternal nature. She could see that no one was doing anything to help me and I was obviously in a very bad way. She knew Miss Jolly, the headmistress, would know what to do but she lived in the town. So once school was over, she broke all the rules and risking her all, ran out of the school through the town to where she knew Miss Jolly lived. She told her there was a real emergency at the school and would she please come quickly – little Hamish was desperately ill, worsening by the minute and the matron had simply put him to bed saying that a good sleep would make him feel better. Miss Jolly knew that no pupil would ever have dared to run away from school unless there had been a real crisis. She responded immediately and rang the emergency services for an ambulance, put on her coat and ran back to the school with the girl. I was rushed to the infirmary with only minutes to spare. I will never forget the journey in the ambulance, it seemed to take a very long time even though it was little more than a mile. I remember a mask being put over my face – and being given a small amount of gas to relieve the pain. I had no idea what was happening, I was so young and so critically ill that I hadn't the strength to fight back. As soon as the ambulance arrived at the hospital I was rushed in for an emergency operation. I had been diagnosed as having acute appendicitis. I owe my life to this girl's courage.

My mother was quickly informed of my situation by the school. As soon as she heard the news, she knew she would have to leave at once for Aberdeen to be with me. She was aware that I would be frightened by the strange hospital surroundings and smells and wouldn't understand the doctors and nurses – she had to get to me at the earliest opportunity but travelling in wartime was fraught with difficulties and despite her best efforts, it took three days before she eventually got to the hospital. When I turned to see her walk in to the ward, I was astonished, delighted, relieved and confused all at the same time. At last I began to feel safe – my mother was here with me. I knew she would help me to understand what was going on, why I was here, why I had a huge bandage round my middle and why I felt so uncomfortable. In view of the difficulty the hospital staff had communicating with me, my mother was allowed to stay until I was fully recovered. Although hospital meant soreness, horrible-tasting medicines and sometimes nurses sticking needles into me, now that my mother was with me I felt happier. As I began to recover and regain my strength my many aunts and cousins came to visit me and I almost felt that being in hospital was better than being at school! Within a few weeks I was discharged and returned to school to recuperate where all my classmates were very interested in what had happened to me and ghoulishly wanted to see my bandages and 'wounds'. I quite enjoyed being the centre of attention, but it was short-lived. My 'wounds' slowly turned painfully septic and two weeks later I was taken back to the infirmary for a further operation to 'clean me up'. The school holidays had just started when I finally left Aberdeen Infirmary, so my mother came to take me back to South Ronaldsay for a second recuperative spell. Going home by boat was the best medicine I could have been given – I already felt much better!

I sailed on the ss St Magnus many times between school and home. It took my mother and I to Kirkwall from Aberdeen Infirmary. The boat was old and primitive.

CHAPTER 6　　*Happy Times*

My mother found herself completely alone once I had gone away to school and my father was away in the war. Hameneuk must have seemed very empty. My grandfather in Wick was quite concerned about her being left totally on her own and so decided to buy her a dog. I remember the excitement at coming back from school one holiday and finding Laddie, who was good company for my mother when she was on her own.

Me, holding our dog Laddie

The Aberdeen Special School for the Deaf and the Orkney school holidays never coincided. So there were long periods when I spent a lot of time with my mother and playing on my own. I came to really value this time as it turned out to be my only real experience of childhood play. During this time, I would set up my clockwork train and my toy cars. My mother allowed me to cover the floor of four rooms so I could make a really big layout and take it into my inner world. There I was in sole charge and there were no communication barriers. My imaginary characters knew my thoughts and understood my words. I created and took charge of the 'Hameneuk District' road and rail network. It is difficult to describe how much I missed these precious hours when I was away at boarding school. They gave me a much needed opportunity to learn to come to terms with myself and my thoughts after the rigour and tightly timetabled routine of my Aberdeen school.

When I was six years old, in 1946, something totally unexpected happened during the holidays. One day, my mother dressed us both up to go out. I assumed that this heralded a visit to one of my mother's friends but to my surprise, my father's erstwhile boss, the sub-postmaster, arrived shortly afterwards to collect us in his car. I had no idea where he was taking us but going out was quite fun and a ride in a car an additional treat. He drove us down to the harbour in Kirkwall. There was always lots of interesting activity to watch there but today something different seemed to be going on. Lots of people, mostly women, were standing around on the quayside looking as if they were waiting for something. My mother and I got out of the car to join the crowd and she lifted me up so that I could see what was going on. We stood waiting for quite a while but I couldn't see anything special happening. Then she suddenly pointed to the big, dark outline of a boat sailing in towards the harbour. I could feel the excitement rising in her and began to sense that the trip to the harbour and the incoming boat meant something out of the ordinary. All around us the women started to jump up and down waving their hands more and more excitedly as the boat got nearer and nearer and my mother joined in with them and encouraged me to wave with her. I remember seeing the tall funnel belching out clouds of black smoke as the boat very, very slowly approached the harbour. As it got nearer, I could see people on the deck waving back to us and my mother quickly turning to me saying "Daddy, Hamish that's your Daddy – he's come home," pointing to my long lost father standing on deck wearing, of all things, a bush hat! He, too, was waving frantically knowing that my mother would be there to meet him. When I saw her say – 'Daddy', to me and point to the boat several times, it took me a few minutes to realise what she meant. Could she really mean that my 'Daddy' was really coming home after what seemed to me like a life-time. When he finally stepped off the boat with all the other servicemen and fought his way through the crowd to my mother and I, it was a very emotionally charged moment. She wept tears of joy and relief as we all hugged each other. She had hardly dared even to think about the possibility of his return ever since he left and I had grown used to my father's inexplicable disappearance – the idea of him ever returning home never entered my head. We were driven back to Hameneuk and a period of getting to know each other again, including the new member of the

Welcoming my father home from the war in Burma
via Hong Kong, 1946. One of the greatest surprise in
all my life.

family – Laddie, our dog. I hoped my father would never 'disappear' again, now that he had come home.

He was quite surprised to see that the toddler he had left behind had grown into a real little boy. Although he noticed a considerable physical change in my appearance on his return, he saw very little progress in my oral communication. I still had no knowledge of speech after my two years away at the Aberdeen Special School for the Deaf, but my mother knew how important it was to keep the long term goal in mind and not allow discouragement to creep in.

After the war was over and my father left the army, he went back to his job as postman and life began to slowly return to normal. I hated going back to school even more now that my father was home. But at least he was there when I came home in the holidays. In the summer months I enjoyed playing out in the open with a small homemade tent that I used to put up in the garden near our chicken coop and pretend I was camping. It was fun to sit inside and watch the chickens strutting about in the garden, pecking at the grass. I grew very fond of one in particular – she became quite tame and let me stroke her rich brown feathers. They were smooth and warm to the touch. Once I was playing in my tent when, to my delight, she walked up, stopped momentarily, before peering right inside and then promptly walked straight in up to me to be given her customary stroke! She seemed very reluctant to return to the other chickens out in the garden.

Animals seemed to sense that I had absolutely no fear of them which meant that I could get very close to them as I did with Laddie. Laddie was with us for many years and he and I became great friends. One school holiday the next-door neighbours' dog, a German spaniel, and Laddie got into a vicious fight in a mad moment. Laddie was almost torn to pieces. I was playing at the bottom of our road when I happened to look up and saw the two dogs locked in battle. As I ran up the hill to try to separate them, the neighbours' dog made a very quick escape the moment he saw me approaching. Laddie was so badly savaged that he was barely alive. He couldn't move, so I picked him up and carried him into the kitchen at Hameneuk. My mother and I kept him warm and did our best to try to make him comfortable until my father came home from work. There was no vet on the island at the time and as Laddie was in such a terrible state he decided to drive him down to a farm in the South Parish which belonged to a fellow postman, and took me with him. His colleague knew immediately what had to be done to put the poor dog out of his misery. I can still see him taking great care to aim his gun with great precision. I couldn't hear the shot but I saw the kick of the gun and the sudden slump of Laddie's body. It was very sad – I knew my companion had gone.

Despite the difference in the school holiday dates, I managed to make one or two good friends on the island. I would go to their houses to play and they would come to Hameneuk as did my two cousins, Zena and Alister. We somehow managed to communicate with each other through simple gestures when we played together but if my mother was with me, she would often speak to my friends on my behalf. She really was the person who best understood me but I often became intensely frustrated because although I knew my mother had done her best to communicate for me, I could see by my friends' reaction that she had not understood entirely what I wanted to say. Toys were hard to come by during, and for some time after, the war, so many household objects doubled for the purpose of play – saucepans and wooden spoons became drums and drumsticks, upturned tables were transformed into sailing ships, cardboard boxes became cosy little beds for much-loved teddies and so on. I was more fortunate than most of the children on the island in that my father made me marvellous toys from bits and pieces in his workshop. A particular one I remember was a small wooden tricycle made from scrap wood and old pram wheels.

My father made this tricycle. It even had a front brake. Me and Billy Banks having a great time!

Perhaps my favourite holiday activity was playing football with a real leather football, particularly after the soft, woolly pompom ball games in the school playground in Aberdeen. One summer holiday I became the proud owner of a pair of hard-toed football boots and felt very professional in them. I had seen the St Margaret's Hope football team play. Their goalkeeper was daring and brilliant and immediately became my hero. I think he also worked as a fishmonger in between being a brilliant goalkeeper and travelled round the islands in a small white van. He also ran a fish and chip shop in St Margaret's Hope which opened occasionally, usually on Saturdays, for a couple of hours. I would sit at home and watch the clock, waiting for opening time and then run down the hill to the delicious smells that came from his shop eager to have the chance to 'speak' to my hero in person before taking the weekly treat of fish and chips home.

My dream was to learn to be as good a goalkeeper as my hero. But there was no opportunity at school, and much of my father's time was necessarily taken up with his work, so Bob Gunn, an old friend of his and neighbour, took his place and kindly gave me a game now and then.

On my return to South Ronaldsay, I very much wanted my friends, Bob and Maggie, to meet Bob Gunn and his wife, Margaret. I remember them as lovely neighbours from my childhood. So, one day, we drove down to Herston, a tiny collection of peaceful houses that look out across the water, where they now lived. I knocked on their door and, despite being overwhelmed by such an unexpected visit, they both greeted us with delight. "Oh, he's so tall, oh my, just look at him, oh dear, I remember him as a small boy with curly hair," I saw her tell Maggie, as she took us inside to the sitting room. She bustled about making tea and arranging cakes and shortbread on her best three-tier cake stand before joining us. The tea was poured out and she began to share some of her memories of me with Maggie. "He used to come up and visit us very often and he would make noises, you know, we used to think it was so sad that he couldn't say the words. He was such a lovely little boy with his curly hair . . . oh, it was a shame, you see it wasn't really normal." I could see what she was saying from across the room. I had no idea of the sad little picture I had apparently presented to her. My "childhood noises," as she referred to them, had long since developed into a small voice and speech that astonished her. She told me of her deep thrill at seeing me chatting confidently and animatedly to her husband. It hardly seemed possible to her that so much had developed from virtually nothing. "You know, his mother had to give him up to the special school in Aberdeen when he was only four years old, to give him a chance of making his way in the wide world," she told Maggie, "Oh, that must have been a terrible thing to do, but so brave, you know. It was very difficult to understand it then, but now it is clear why it had to be done. Real vision his mother had to do that and just look what rewards it has brought him." Bob Gunn and I reminisced about the times in St Margaret's Hope when I 'played' football with him. We first set up a

makeshift goal in his front garden and then we would start the game. Following in the footsteps of my hero, I was always in goal, and saving a shot gave me a great sense of achievement. Bob would patiently show me different moves and techniques which I learned to imitate.

One of my great Orkney childhood friends was Billy Banks. He lived close by to Hameneuk and we used to play football together whenever parts of our school holidays coincided. My clockwork train set held a great fascination for him. We would sit together on the floor playing for hours at a time and very little communication was needed. Billy had a great love of the sea and had a little dinghy of his own. I remember how, one summer day, he managed to coax me into it. Although we had played in his dinghy before,

Terrific experience. Billy Banks took me in his dingy to Scapa Flow — not far into it but the sea was black. I wanted to go back home sooner but my pride stopped me!

I was less confident about small boats than he. My experience of boats had been travelling on the ferry between Orkney and the mainland of Scotland. These ferries were big enough to give me a sense of security which Billy's small dinghy lacked. As he started to row the dinghy away from the safety of the shore, I fought the terror mounting in me, determined not to show it. The further out he rowed the more exposed and vulnerable I felt. It seemed to me that we had gone right out beyond the boundary of the 'Hope past the headland towards Scapa Flow! Although this had the makings of a great adventure, I was petrified by this time, and wondering if we would ever get back to St Margaret's Hope again. Like most boys, I enjoyed exploring and adventures but I rarely launched very far into the unknown. I preferred the safety of known boundaries.

I decided to take my friends with me to visit Billy the following afternoon on the off chance that he might be at home. He and his wife gave us all a warm welcome and we spent some time talking over old times and exchanging news of what each of us was now doing. I was fascinated to learn from Billy that he had no recollection of having any communication difficulties with me when we played together. He had maintained his love of the sea and before his retirement, had spent many years operating his ferry business between John O'Groats and Burwick in South Ronaldsay.

We left Billy's home and walked up towards Hameneuk to look across to the back of the village to a small workshop where, during a particularly long summer break, I spent many hours with the local joiner. After years of watching my father repairing and making things in his workshop at Hameneuk, I began to want to make things myself. My father was keen for me to see a real craftsman at work so took me to the joinery. I got to know James Omand, the joiner, who was very skilled, and loved to watch him at work on his bench surrounded by all sorts of interesting work in progress. There was a great sense of activity, and he never seemed to tire of my many visits. The floor was covered in sawdust and shavings and there was always a wonderful smell of new wood in the air. We managed to communicate with each other in a very basic way – he must have been extremely patient with me. During this long summer break, when I was about eleven years old, he asked me if I would like to make something myself. I was very excited by the idea and indicated that I would really like to make an ironing board for my mother. I went to his workshop almost daily for the next few weeks. James first helped me to cut the wood to size and plane it to the right thickness. It then had to be cut to the appropriate size. After that he showed me how to sand all the components to a really smooth finish so as to prevent my mother getting a splinter in her hand. The various pieces were then carefully assembled, glued and pinned together. I remember the very particular smell of the wood glue bubbling away in its kettle on a small gas ring in the corner of the workshop – it was the colour of liquid toffee. The finished ironing board was then left to set. I was very pleased with the quite professional looking result of my efforts although it was rather heavy. At least it was solid and would last a long time and a few days later, I proudly presented it to her. She was most impressed with my handiwork and, despite its weight and awkward handling, stoically used it for a good ten years probably out of loyalty, I suspect.

As we walked down to the 'Hope, we passed the pier road. It holds a very special memory for me. During another of my school holidays, I was deeply engrossed in playing, when my mother indicated that she wanted me to walk down to the 'Hope with her. I was quite annoyed at having my play interrupted and could not imagine why she wanted me to go with her, but she was so persistent that I reluctantly agreed to leave my toys and go along. As we approached the bottom of the hill, I could see a man on a bicycle riding towards us along the pier road. But something was not quite right about the scene. As the man and bicycle got nearer and nearer I saw, to my astonishment, that the man was sitting perched precariously on the handle bars facing the wrong way, riding the bicycle backwards! As he cycled past us, I was even more taken aback to see that the man was in fact my father! I was very impressed by his skill, but I could not work out why he would want to do such a thing. What did it mean? It turned out to be my father's unique surprise

Hesston village where Bob and Margaret Gunn lived and
my grandmother retired. Two of my aunts and an uncle also
lived there. The escaping flame of Flotta's oil terminal is in
the distance.

presentation of a new bicycle for me. I was stunned – not only to be given my very own bicycle, but a brand new one, a beautiful Triumph; something that I had never imagined not even in my wildest dreams. No wonder my mother had been so insistent that I go with her!

My mother enjoyed having me at home during the holidays, but she never once let slip the important task of continuing my communication education. She knew how essential it was not to let all the hard work of the school term fade away. In order to support this, she travelled to Aberdeen, to meet with my teachers to see how she could help further my communication skills during the school breaks. They invited her to observe the speech therapist working with me, so that she could carry on aspects of the training with me at home. There was to be no respite for me, but at least I would be working at home with my mother and far from my tyrannical school across the water. She was also very keen for me to learn to enjoy reading, knowing it would enable me to gain a great deal of knowledge to which I would otherwise not have access. Hearing children could 'pick up' information and facts aurally, but everything I needed to know would have to be learnt or read. Learning to read was yet another arduous task and I found little joy in reading with my limited language. I can remember my mother trying very hard to explain to me the importance of good reading and how to read – I was not just to scan over a page picking up a few words or a sentence here and there, but was to read a single sentence at a time, over and over again until I understood it clearly before moving on. In this way I would slowly build up the whole story. During a visit to my grandparents in Wick, she bought me my first serious book – an abridged version of *The Thirty Nine Steps* by John Buchan, but tackling it was a real chore. It took me many, many years to learn to enjoy reading. I preferred doing things like painting and drawing where I could get more instant results with a visual language rather than with a written or spoken one.

Although it seemed that I lived in a world of silence, my mother felt that there might have been a slender chance of my having a shred of residual hearing. So whenever any rhythmic Scottish dance music was broadcast, she would sit me right up against the radio with my ear touching the mesh of the speaker and the volume turned right up. Even if I could not actually hear any sound at all, my mother knew I would at least be able to feel and learn to enjoy the rhythmic vibrations. It was a tremendous thrill to experience this. Today I still love to 'hear' music with a strong rhythmic base through the feel of the vibrations. Some years ago, Bob and Maggie took me to 'listen' to their son's band, Gamut, playing. The club atmosphere was alive and I felt the same excitement as I did as a child, following the deep beat with no trouble at all. As anyone could see – my foot automatically tapped in time to what they told me was almost painfully loud music to them. My poor hearing friends looked as though they were really suffering!

Despite being quite curious about the nature of sound, I think I would be terrified if I were to suddenly have my hearing restored. As I have never known what it is, I have nothing to compare it with and can only conjecture about it. I have only ever known profound deafness and though I have known one or two hearing people feel sorry for me, I have to remind them that I cannot feel the loss of something I have never known.

A few days after renewing my acquaintance with Billy, we went to visit the Tomb of the Eagles – a recently excavated cairn, discovered on a farm where another of my school holiday friends, Shirley, used to live. Both our fathers worked at the sub post office in St Margaret's Hope and her father owned a farm near Hameneuk. It was he who had put our dog, Laddie, out of his misery after he had been so badly savaged.

I introduced myself to the farmer and was delighted to see that he remembered me. I asked after Shirley and to my surprise learned that, the little girl I remembered, was now married with a family of her own and still lived on the island. She and I played together in the holidays and I remember how she always seemed to be very protective of me.

We were ushered into the tiny museum, converted from part of the farmhouse, to see the extraordinary handling collection of historic artifacts. We then went out to view the burial ground itself. On our return to the farmhouse, I was amazed to find Shirley herself there. One of the family had telephoned her and she had raced over hoping to catch me before we left. We hugged each other and recounted how our lives had changed over nearly fifty years. Shirley had even bothered to bring an old photograph of us both playing in the very spot where we were standing, just as I remembered. It was difficult to believe that she was about to become a grandmother!

My school holidays inevitably came to an end. I always dreaded the new school term. Everything I loved had to be left behind for months on end. However, the one tiny compensation about returning to school was either a boat or plane journey to Aberdeen. I particularly loved flying. It felt very exciting – I could feel the shudder and vibration of the engines. I remember once when it was time for me to leave Orkney for Aberdeen, my father took me to the airport and he had to help the ground crew push the little twin-engined De Havilland aircraft, out of the hangar

The little plane taking me to school in Aberdeen via Wick flew over Hamonewk. My father waving with a white sheet. I could never help bursting into tears. His Royal Mail van is parked in the drive.

on to the runway. I really hated leaving home even though my mother came with me when I was very young. I always got on the plane fighting back the tears and the air crew got to know me very well. The pilot would fly out to sea low, over Hameneuk and I would look out of the window to see my father standing in the garden waving a white hanky. This became a sort of tradition and although I liked to see him way below me, the sight doubly underlined the separation and upset me even more. If only there had been a school for the deaf in Orkney! I expect my mother was equally sad at our partings but she hid it from me. As far as I was concerned, I was just being sent back to what felt more or less like a lonely prison but I grew to know that every so often the school holidays came around and my mother would come over by boat to collect me and take me back to my beloved island. After I was eight years old, I was allowed to travel home on my own and was even trusted to make my own way from the school to the harbour to catch the boat back to Orkney. I am quite amazed thinking about it now. I was the only boy in the school who the matron ever really trusted. She saw that I had learned to be responsible and dependable and, unlike some of the other boys, would rarely put myself at risk.

I remember one or two trips back to school being special. Bob Gunn, our neighbour, sometimes took me back to school. We travelled all the way from South Ronaldsay in his very smart black Jaguar which had real leather upholstery with a wonderful smell. I felt very important sitting beside him as we sped smoothly on our way, even though we were heading for Aberdeen and school. I loved to see the countryside flashing past us, but I secretly wished that Bob would drive just a little slower. I had no wish to get back to school any earlier than absolutely necessary! On one of these occasions, my wish was granted. The smooth ride was abruptly interrupted by a series of sharp, extremely uncomfortable bumps and the car began to swerve around in the road. I wondered what could have happened and anxiously looked out of the window to see what was going on. To my great surprise and amusement, I saw one of Bob's prize Jaguar wheels gently rolling away from the car on to the roadside! Fortunately there was very little traffic around and he was able to manoeuvre his then three-wheeled car off the road to safety. He explained to me that it was too late to find a garage to repair the car that day and that we would have to stay the night in a hotel. Later that evening, Bob explained that this was the result of a broken shaft. To this day I can remember the thrill of the adventure, particularly as it meant my return to school being unavoidably delayed – it was marvellous!

Happy Times

CHAPTER 7 *My Father*

During my visit back to my island, I took my friends up to Harrabrough Head. We passed Little Myre, the croft where my father was born and grew up. Years ago I used to pass it on my way up through the fields to the sheer cliffs of the Head where I went to watch the birds. I would spend hours up there, sitting very still, almost at the edge of the cliff, to get a good view of the birds flying below me, but high above the crashing waves. Every so often one or two would fly up above where I was sitting so that I could see their feet tucked up against their bodies as they rode on the wind. Being so close to them always gave me a sense of exhilaration. Up there I was alone with the birds and my thoughts, far away from the constant struggle of trying to make myself understood or trying to understand others. I felt free. Looking back, I realise how lucky I was to be allowed to go off on my own like that. My mother must have been very trusting to give me such independence. I find it quite difficult to imagine how I ever managed to avoid the potential dangers of such freedom, but I did, despite my total deafness.

As we walked along, I began to share, with Bob and Maggie, what my father had told me about life on the island in his time. Learning about his background has helped me understand something of what fuelled his unusual enterprise and resourcefulness. I am sure that my own 'DIY' ability comes from hours of watching him work as a child. I learned a lot of skills in this way. The difference between us now is that his enterprise and energy continues whereas, I am rather ashamed to say, mine dwindles as I get older and am more inclined to pay 'professionals' to do the work for me! Since my mother died in 1988, he has lived on his own in their maisonette in Surrey, looking after himself and seeing to odd jobs for his neighbours. His whole life has been, and still is, about making good, practical use of discarded items. In the garden, for instance, he has adapted a

Little Myre where my father was born. He was last of seven children. Little Myre was a small croft.

large, glass coffee jar to serve as a protective cover for his outside light. Old copper piping has been bent and appropriately flattened to form useful hand rails outside his kitchen door and the cross head from a bath tap serves as an easy-to-grip door handle to his greenhouse. There is no practical task to which he can't turn his hand. His personal endeavour, has significantly influenced my life and I have learned the value of application, organisation and punctuality from his example.

My father is the only survivor of his three brothers and four sisters. He was educated at the Widewall school in the South Parish (in South Ronaldsay) until he was fourteen but, to use his own words, he "never felt there was much going on there!" He was more practical than academic and preferred making things, helping his father at Little Myre and trying to repair things around the house for his mother. This often proved extremely difficult as there was no money for even the most basic tools.

Little Myre consisted of land, a barn, a byre (cow-shed) and a steading (farm building) all of which originally had thatched roofs, a house with two rooms upstairs and two downstairs (one of which was the kitchen) and a small closet on each floor. My father managed to turn one of these into his first tiny workshop. The 'family bathroom' consisted of a hand basin in the kitchen with a tiny mirror above it for shaving. Everyone and everything was washed there. The water had to be fetched from the well three or four times a day as there was no running water in the house. There was no toilet either in or outside – not even a 'dry' one for many years. The byre had to serve this purpose. By the time I was ten and old enough to visit Little Myre on my own, facilities had greatly improved. A smart 'sentry box' had been erected in the yard. This modern convenience consisted of a simple wooden seat with a bucket underneath which gave my poor grandmother the rather unpleasant chore of emptying it daily! The furniture too, was very basic – I remember a very comfortable green leather bench seat from a car doubling as a sofa.

Beyond Little Myre, stands a small church hall. My father still remembers the little song he sang there when he was six years old. When Maggie and I met with him recently, he sang it for her after more than eighty years. I watched him 'singing,' his face alight, his hands moving in time to the rhythm, he was as animated as he must have been when he was a boy. I was very impressed with his memory and very interested to learn what it sounded like.

When my grandfather died of concussion after being kicked by one of his horses, my father pleaded with his mother to let him leave school at eleven so that he too, could help with the croft. However his school teacher advised his mother that, to give up his education at that point, would considerably limit his opportunities for employment in the future and be a very short term solution to helping his mother. So reluctantly, he moved on to the higher school in St Margaret's Hope. He was, however, able to help his mother a little during the school holidays by continuing to work in the fields or breaking up stones for the road. That job meant sitting on a rolled-up sack for forty five minutes at a time chipping off a bit from one side of the stone, turning it over and taking some more off the other side. It was a thankless task. The local blue stones were hard as iron and wore the tips of his fingers out and all for half a crown (twelve and a half pence) per cubic yard of broken stones. But it was much needed income. When the neeps (turnips) needed singling, my father would work a twelve hour day, also for just half a crown. Farmers had little sympathy for young workers like my father. They would place them between two old, experienced hands and then stand over them to make sure they got the maximum out of them.

The Boys' Ploughing Match, an event that is still held annually on South Ronaldsay, was something to which my father always looked forward. It was a real occasion for him. The event is held on the Sands O'Right where boys under fifteen years of age, decorated and dressed up as 'horses' complete with mock halters, enter the competition and plough a small area of the sands with miniature ploughs. It is quite an art. The results are then formally judged and medals awarded. My father's skill once won him one of these coveted medals.

Shortly after my father left the school in St Margaret's Hope, he got a job in the Post Office shop at ten shillings a week. Jobs were few and far between on such a small island and highly valued so my father felt very privileged. He started work at the counter and also did a post round if one of the postmen was away. He very much enjoyed this aspect of his job. It gave him a greater sense of responsibility and an opportunity to prove himself. A couple of years later, when a vacancy for a postman arose, my father successfully applied for the job. He started off by doing two rounds, one to Hoxa and the other to Grimness, on foot or bicycle, every other day.

Work started at the Post Office at nine in the morning and finished at half past two in the afternoon for my father. He then went to work with his brother James, at Rosie's Garage – a car hire and taxi business they ran between them. They had two cars for hire and ran a fourteen-seater bus service to take people into St Margaret's Hope to do their shopping. The business really needed more of my father's time to expand it, so he set about getting hold of a motorcycle to cut down the time his rounds took. He eventually managed to get a New Imperial motorbike sent up from Scotland, to use for his Post Office work, but it was very much against the rules and he had to take out his own insurance.

After the war, my father was given a brand new, bright red post van and he often helped people out by running errands for them although, strictly speaking, that was not permitted either. He once helped one of his customers out by taking his three sheep in the back of the post van from one farm to another for him – across open fields! The farmer was delighted by this kindness. But that was, and still is, typical of my father's generosity with his time.

When I was home from school and old enough, I often went with my father to help him at the Post Office. Sometimes I helped with sorting the mail, making sure the right letters were put in the right bags ready for delivery and I was allowed to help with franking the mail with a special stamp. One of my favourite jobs was helping to tie up the bags of outgoing mail and fastening them with the special lead seal that read "St Margaret's Hope" ready to be driven by my father to Kirkwall on their way to mainland Scotland. On other occasions, I went with him in the van on his rounds and I can still remember the lovely smell of the canvas mail bags in the back.

During snowstorms in the cold, Orkney winters, deliveries were far from straightforward. When the roads were completely blocked and blizzards were blowing, my father would have to leave his van and make his way along the top of the dykes (dry stone walls) in order to get a letter to a customer. He took great pride in his work. He had a duty to fulfill and had no intention of ever failing to do so. When I went with him in my winter holidays, I would be sent out through the deep snow in one direction to deliver a letter whilst he went in the other – nothing ever stood in the way of his delivery. In those conditions, the round took hours to finish but it was always completed however bad the weather. The cold was so intense one year, that my father got severe frostbite in his right ear and lost part of it. My mother knew how loyal my father was to his employer and worried about him being out in the freezing weather for hours on end.

There were only a few postboxes on the island at that time, so my father sometimes made private arrangements for collections with individuals who would 'pay' him in kind for his trouble. At Christmas time he would be inundated with offerings of hens, ducks and a whole range of other produce. He often had to ask his generous customers to keep some of them until at least February as he had far more than he could possibly get through! During the festive season, his many appreciative customers would also insist he take a drink with them. There were often so many of these invitations to accept that these festive toasts often extended into March!

Some years after the war, my father went down to Edinburgh with a local farmer to take his sheep to market. When he was there, he bought a big, second-hand Fiat – a seven seater Laundaulet with five gears and a folding seat in the back. He paid thirty-five pounds for it and intended hiring it out as a hearse through Rosie's Garage – an alternative to the local horse-drawn hearse. He and the farmer brought it back on the boat with them and sat in it with all the doors open, thoroughly enjoying the grandeur. When it was hired out as a hearse, my father would put two empty egg crates in the back for the coffin to lie on and keep it from sliding. It lasted a good many years and took a number of people to their funerals with great dignity. When it finally came to an end, my father who, with his upbringing, could never see anything go to waste, typically converted it into a tractor! He cut the chassis down and attached a couple of big wheels from old reaping machines sent up to him by boat from an Aberdeen scrap merchant. After the success of this unusual conversion, one or two old cars he had at the garage were also cut down and transformed into tractors. All this was done long before commercial tractors were available on the island.

On a recent visit to the Tankerness House Museum in Kirkwall, I came across a photograph of an unusual-looking car. I knew exactly who the owner and designer was – my own father! I had heard all about this car and how he had built it single-handed. The fact that he was busy casting blocks with which to build Hameneuk, working for the Post Office and Rosie's Garage in no way deterred him from starting another project. He had seen the first part of a series of plans for a 'DIY' three-wheeler published in a magazine. He had been thinking along similar lines some while back. The first plan was for a wooden chassis which set my father thinking. He knew of an old, burnt out Austin Seven which he managed to salvage and use as an alternative to a wooden chassis. He cut the body away and through the rear member so that he could draw the sides together to fit a single rear wheel. He then fitted narrow strips of larch wood along the chassis which he steamed into shape along the back before fixing them into position. My father dismantled an AJS engine from an old motorbike and sidecar and reassembled it to fit on the one rear wheel. The gear lever

My father built this car from plans using bits of an old car and motor cycle!

and the handbrake were mounted and operated on the exterior of the body. The brake for the rear wheel was operated by a foot pedal. The car had a kick-start, no dynamo, battery or lights so could only be used in daylight hours. There was nothing under the bonnet, except the driver's and passenger's feet. The body was made of a wooden frame covered with sheets of zinc and held together by hundreds of quarter inch screws which all had to be put in by hand – there were no electric screwdrivers then. He made the mudguards from iron rods that he bent, shaped, squeezed together and covered in zinc. The body work was finally painted brown with paint left over from painting the doors at Hameneuk and a radiator was faked with strips of cut zinc, just for show. There was no roof or canopy over the car – it was of the 'sporting' type and permanently open.

My father proudly gave his fiancé the first run out in his homemade car and recalled that it was quite a tight fit and a bit of a courting car! He managed to keep it on the road for a full two years. At the end of its life, it was typically recycled. My father removed the engine and gave the shell to a friend for his son to play with.

I made a point of going to tell the museum curator that I not only knew who the owner was, but also its history.

I have always been a keen birdwatcher. My mother allowed me to wander round high cliff edges, looking for birds.

My Father

CHAPTER 8

My Mother

My mother was a very special person with real foresight for me. She became as much my teacher as my mother, and she never gave up her hope for me. Christina, as she was named, was born and grew up in Wick. She came from a very disciplined and hard-working family and was the second of four children – two girls and two boys and her small stature earned her the nickname 'Tiny.' Her parents had a high regard for education and training and were keen for all their children to gain qualifications and have a profession. It was impossible for my grandfather to finance all four of his children through college, so the family agreed a system of shared responsibility that would enable them all to benefit from further education. It worked as follows: my grandfather paid for his eldest child to train as a nurse with the proviso that she had to save enough money from her employment to pay for her sister's training as a teacher. This was my mother, and her responsibility was to pay for her eldest brother's training as a pharmacist and, in turn, he had to pay for his younger brother who also wanted to train in pharmacy. At the end of his training, he had to repay my grandfather's initial outlay.

When it came to my mother's turn to go to college, she went to train as a teacher at Moray House in Edinburgh. She successfully completed her course during the bleak days of the 1930's Depression when jobs were very scarce for men, and practically non-existent for women. My mother had no choice over jobs – she had to take the first offer that came her way as she had a duty to start saving for her brother's training. So when she was offered the appointment of resident teacher on the the tiny island of Copinsay in Orkney, she had no hesitation in accepting it. The need for a teacher arose from there being an unusual number of children on the island – twenty-five – belonging to three families. Fourteen belonged to Copinsay's only farmer and the other eleven to the three lighthouse keepers, the only other residents on the island.

Unfortunately, Maggie, my biographer, never met my mother. There would have been much that she could have told her about me from a mother's perspective. But that was not to be. The best we could do was to visit, Mollie King, a very good friend of my mother's who knew her from her teaching days on South Ronaldsay. Mollie had been a teacher herself at the school in St Margaret's Hope so she and my mother had a lot in common. "Mrs Mollie" as I knew her, frequently visited Hameneuk and has known me all my life.

We drove over to Kirkwall one afternoon, to have tea with her. "Tiny was a wonderful mother and friend," Mollie told us, "she had a great sense of humour and a lovely singing voice. Of course she was very worried about Hamish's loss of hearing, but her determination to pave the way

The Hope school where my mother was a 'support' teacher. Mollie King also taught there. I could see it from my bedroom window at Hameneuk.

for him never wavered. She knew how to get on with whatever had to be done – she had no time for self-pity and I know Hamish has followed in her footsteps. I remember you, Hamish, being a very single-minded little boy. Once, when you had all come over for tea, I put a clean, white cloth on the table with a special place mat on top for you, so that it didn't matter if you made a mess. When you sat up to the table, you very obviously indicated that you did not want a special mat. You had noticed that the grown-ups never had mats and had no intention of being treated differently! Little incidents like that were a great encouragement to your mother. They showed how you very definitely thought for yourself even if you could not communicate what you wanted to say."

My mother used to tell me about the island where she had lived and worked and often pointed out the flashing beam of the Copinsay lighthouse from the kitchen window at Hameneuk. I was fascinated by what she told me but I could never fully picture the island, the lighthouse or the schoolroom where she taught. I always dreamt of going there one day to see it for myself.

By an extraordinary coincidence we discovered, that whilst we were in Orkney, there was to be a reunion of the Groat family who had once lived and farmed on Copinsay. The fourteen children had all been taught by my mother, and seven of them were to return to the island for the reunion. Through an article in *The Orcadian* newspaper they had learned about our visit and how I was their former teacher's son. They very kindly asked my friends and I to join them on their trip back to Copinsay. It was difficult to believe that after all these years, I was unexpectedly to visit this tiny island and even meet some of my mother's very first pupils and learn something about her teaching days and life on the island. Though my mother told me many times about her time on Copinsay, I knew very little of the detail. I don't have the opportunity to slowly 'absorb' history or information over time as hearing people do. Casual talk and detail pass me by. My sense of history has to be gained from books or face to face conversation with another. Acquiring information is a far more deliberate process for a deaf person.

On a bright morning, we met up with the seven 'children' (now in their seventies and eighties) by the old church at the Bay of Skaill in Deerness and, to our astonishment, found that four generations of the family were to join the reunion and cross to the island to see where their forbears had lived. Two fishing boats and an inflatable outboard were waiting alongside the rough stone jetty to take the entire gathering – more than forty of the family, and ourselves in relays across to Copinsay! It was apparently almost sixty years to the day that, due to the father's ill health, the Groat family had left their island home. Their return to Copinsay was to be as memorable for them as my first visit would be. As the boat chugged out to sea, I felt the thrill of the engine vibrating and the salt spray on my face. In the distance I could see the tiny island that I had longed to visit. I knew my mother would have been delighted to know that I was on my way there and would have been so surprised that I was in the company of many of her first pupils. I began to think about how she must have felt all those years ago when she made the very same journey with her bags and school books, on her way out to her very first job. Her feelings must have been rather mixed. She wouldn't have known quite what she was going to and probably wondered what life would be like on such a remote, small island in the North Sea. In those days, Copinsay supported a single farm, a lighthouse and a wealth of bird life. Today the manned lighthouse I used to see from Hameneuk, operates automatically and the island is uninhabited. It has become a designated RSPB bird sanctuary.

Before long, we reached the island and the boat came gently alongside the same little wooden pier where my mother would have disembarked in 1935. It felt strange to be setting foot on the sandy shore just as she had done when she arrived to take up her first teaching post. Standing on the beach with some of her 'school children' was an experience I could never have anticipated. As I stood there, taking the scene in, I learned that nothing had really changed since my mother's time.

We made our way up the grassy bank from the beach to the stone farmhouse where my mother had once worked in the schoolroom. It stood virtually unchanged by time or weather. Slowly the extended family began to gather outside the house. Without exception, the older generation all remembered their teacher – 'Miss Henderson' with affection. She would have been very touched.

Bessie and her sister, Eva, took us into their former home and explained that the painted, wood-lined room we had walked into had been the schoolroom where my mother had once taught her class. Today, in memory of a famous naturalist, the room is appropriately set up as an education room for the small number of visitors to the island. Originally the wood cladding was unpainted and made the room darker. From the schoolroom window, there was a magnificent view out across the shore to the sea and the sky beyond and I could imagine my mother looking out of the same window, seeing the view change dramatically in many different weather conditions.

Orkney bird life.

The Groat family began to give me details of my mother's routine in the schoolroom. On bitter, winter days my mother would stand by the blackboard, her back to an open fire, facing the children sitting at tables. The entire school consisted of a single class. All the children were taught together irrespective of age differences. The various textbooks my mother used were kept in recessed cupboards either side of the fireplace. They were the same as those used in schools on the Mainland. As Bessie began to explain how the school room had originally been set out, a picture slowly formed in my mind. I could almost see my mother standing there teaching her large rather disparate class to read, write and master basic arithmetic. She was responsible for teaching a whole range of subjects including poetry, music, sewing and art. "When it came to art, we all thought Miss Henderson was a real artist, she was so clever at drawing and painting. We were all hopeless!" Bessie told me. She went on to tell how my mother always started the school day with the Lord's Prayer and one verse of a hymn. I wondered if she did this because of her own deep faith and the absence of a church on the island. Ordinary school lessons then followed and every Friday afternoon, she taught her class about the Bible from a special book of her own. My mother's lovely singing voice was something that all the sisters remembered very well. She made sure they too, learned to sing properly and taught them the rudiments of music from the blackboard. Sometimes when Mrs Groat was working in the kitchen and heard my mother singing with her class, she would ask her to go through afterwards so that she could listen more closely herself.

In the summer, my mother would sometimes take her class out to a flattish area behind the byres that are still standing at the back of the house and teach the children to play

Copinsay farmhouse – apart from the lighthouse, it is the only house on the island, now owned by RSPB in memory of a well known naturalist.

rounders. That was where the school picnics were held. "The teacher we had before your mother, was horrid. We really disliked her", Bessie recalled, "so when Miss Henderson arrived, it was lovely. She had such a pleasant personality, we all liked her very much even though she never stood for any

A view to the west from Copinsay Lighthouse. You can see the lone farmhouse at the bottom of the island. South Ronaldsay is on far left in the background.

nonsense. No one was ever allowed to quarrel and she made sure that we all behaved ourselves. But because she was such a nice person, we all wanted to be good and please her. It was a wonderful life, paddling about, swimming in the sea sometimes several times a day in the summer and making daisy chains. We spent hours like that when school was over."

There was never any hope of any real outdoor games in winter as the short days were gale torn, wet and raw. Copinsay never had much snow or frost. The wet, winter gales cut through everything and howled up the side of the farmhouse on wild days. Winds whipped up the sea into great waves that crashed in against the rocks below the lighthouse where my mother lived. The wind would blow the spray right up over the cliffs which then poured down on to the island like driving rain. It was often difficult to tell the difference between real rain and spray.

We followed Bessie, and Eva, through into the rather dark, wood-lined hallway where, on the wall at the foot of the stairs, were the six Groat sisters' coat pegs, just as they had been in the old days. I noticed that above each peg, one of the sisters' names had been scratched into the wood panelling.

Copinsay Lighthouse where my mother lived during her teaching period on the island.

From the hallway we went through into the whitewashed kitchen where there was a hive of activity. Various generations of the family were unpacking the many bags and boxes brought over on the boats, and laying out a virtual feast. Homemade bread, pancakes, butter and cheese – just as they were made in Mrs Groat's day – jams, cake, clootie dumpling and a whole host of other goodies were piled high on the tables in the house. A quantity of special home-brewed beer had been brought across for the strong hearted. A huge kettle was put on a modern Calor Gas ring, to make tea for the more temperate members of the party – the old kitchen range on which Mrs Groat would have made tea for my mother had long since gone.

We then went for a much needed walk across the fields up to the top of the island to the lighthouse compound, where my mother had lived with one of the lighthouse keepers and his wife. The compound was deserted and the whitewashed buildings locked up. But, to actually see the lighthouse that my mother had told me about and which I had seen flashing from Hameneuk all those years ago was thrilling enough for me. Standing up there, little by little, things that I remembered my mother telling me about Copinsay began to fall into place. I felt it must have been quite a lonely place for a young woman straight from college in Edinburgh. She would need her good sense of humour and adventure. There was no entertainment of any kind on the island so the residents had to make their own. Every so often, the schoolroom would become a dance floor and the lighthouse keepers and their wives would go down to the Groats' farmhouse for the evening. My mother who was very fond of dancing, taught them the steps to formation dancing and, accompanied by a gramophone or Mr Groat on his fiddle, they would dance the evening away.

Despite the rigours, life on the island for my mother seemed to me to have been warm and friendly but I learned from Bessie that there were no regrets on my mother's part when her teaching contract came to an end and the time came for her to leave the island. It seemed that, because she didn't have a boyfriend on Copinsay, she was quite glad to leave!

My longing to know about my mother's two years on the island had been more than satisfied as our magical visit to Copinsay drew to an end. But there remained one last surprise for me. While we were all waiting on the beach for the boat to take us back, Sinclair, one of the Groat brothers, told me how he remembered 'Miss Henderson' trying very hard to teach him how to tell the time on her tiny gold wristwatch. I was thrilled to learn this. The watch he mentioned was the very same one that I remember my mother wearing. It had since been given to my eldest daughter Fiona, who, I knew, would be fascinated by this little piece of history about her grandmother's watch.

Meeting the hospitable Groat family and learning about my mother's experiences firsthand had been truly wonderful and had shown me that she had quite clearly proved the value of a rounded education to herself with her first job. As we made our way back to the Bay of Skaill on the Mainland, I began to see how the life of self-sufficiency and independence on Copinsay had helped to shape her character.

Tomison's Academy in South Parish, South Ronaldsay, where my mother had her second teaching post. It is now deserted. The architecture always fascinated me – so symetrical and unusual.

CHAPTER 9   *Into the Hearing World*

My mind was full of thoughts of how my mother's teaching experience had shaped my future. After our memorable visit to Copinsay and with education very much in mind, Maggie was understandably keen to learn about my remaining years at school. So, back at the cottage, I happily recounted memories of my latter years at school in Aberdeen late into the night.

Unlike my mother's aspiration for me, I had a very simple perspective on life – I was perfectly happy at home with my parents so I couldn't understand why I had to leave my island for the rigours of a boarding school. Why wasn't I allowed to stay there with them? I was very confused by having to return to school and couldn't understand why I was sent back there regularly. Why did I have to leave them and return to school where I was often lonely and unhappy? Couldn't my mother see where I was happiest? Why could we only have such short periods of life together? It took me many years of regularly travelling between boarding school in Aberdeen and my island home to work out why I was sent away. It took me almost eleven years until I left the Special School in Aberdeen at fifteen, to begin to realise the importance of education. With very little language and few communication skills, it was very difficult to grasp the significance of events and why certain things happened.

The Special School in Aberdeen only really met the very basic communication and educational needs of deaf children so my mother knew that I would need a higher level of teaching in order to develop any further potential. The headmistress, Miss Jolly, felt that although I was a fairly late developer, I would benefit greatly from being in a more advanced educational environment. She knew the Mary Hare Grammar School for the deaf, in Berkshire in England, had a good reputation and felt I was capable enough to sit the entrance exam. She felt I had a good chance of passing. When the idea was explained to me I was horrified at the notion of having to go to another school that was even further away from my home. By the age of eleven, I was just beginning to grasp the concept of distance and knew that the grammar school in question was so far away that it would take almost two days to get there. That was like the end of the world to me. I simply could not countenance the idea. I also had no idea what an exam was or what it was for. We never had any exams at the Aberdeen school – ability was never tested. What we picked up and retained was very much up to each individual. We learned by rote and example and never had any formal 'academic' testing. My mother tried very hard to encourage me to think about the idea of taking the entrance exam but there was no persuading me. I was not prepared to go any further away from my home. Naturally she was very disappointed, but sensibly respected my feelings. She knew what a hurdle it was just going to the Special School in Aberdeen.

I was so lucky that my mother never gave up hope for me. After my refusal to go no further away from Orkney than Aberdeen, she began to reflect on how she could further my education there. She had never forgotten the comment Stanley Cursiter, the well-known Orcadian artist and limner to the Queen, made to her when my painting was amongst the winners of the children's competition. When she went to collect the prize for me in Kirkwall, he had made a point of telling her he thought my painting showed great promise and that I should be encouraged to develop it. Art was only taught at a very simple level of drawing and painting at the Special School in Aberdeen and as it seemed that my education was to be completed there, my mother set about investigating what could be done to help realise my artistic potential. She wrote to the Local Education Authority in Aberdeen explaining the position and to ask for their advice on what opportunities might be open to me locally. The Authority were not immediately sympathetic and rather harshly took the view that I was fortunate enough to be attending a Special School.

However, spurred on by Stanley Cursiter's remark, my mother persisted in writing to them regularly until, a year or so later, they finally agreed to send their art inspector to at least look at my work, meet me and assess the situation.

The interview with the inspector involved him and Miss Jolly going through my work and asking me a lot of questions with Miss Jolly helping with the communication. Several days later I received a letter from my mother telling me that, following the inspector's visit, he had recommended I attend art classes at the Aberdeen Grammar School for boys as part of my education programme. I would be able to study art in much greater depth there. My mother was delighted at the reward her efforts had brought. The inspector proposed continuing with the essential language and communication lessons at the Special School on three days of the week and attending art, design, craft and history of art and architecture classes at the Grammar School on the other two days. It all sounded very exciting and different to my normal routine but I felt very apprehensive at what it all would mean. I would be the only boy in the Special School going out to a hearing school for lessons. An interview with the Principal of the Grammar School was arranged and my mother came down to go with me. She was keen to meet him and to make sure I understood what was being arranged. At the interview, the Principal expressed his support for the inspector's proposal in theory but openly showed considerable concern over the difficulties that there would inevitably be with my communication. He felt it would be quite a risk to take me on! However, he based his decision on the school inspector's recommendation, and agreed to take me on 'trial' for two days a week. My mother was delighted and felt that this arrangement helped to mitigate my point-blank refusal to sit the Mary Hare Grammar School entrance exam. I was very excited, particularly after I had been shown the art room, but felt extremely nervous at the thought of being the only deaf boy in the midst of a thousand hearing others. I had only ever been amongst deaf boys and girls at school. What would it feel like to be amongst so many boys? Would hearing boys behave the same way as deaf boys? Would I ever be able to make myself understood? Would I understand them? What would they make of me? At that time, there was no communicator or interpreter support for the deaf. They were expected to muddle through alone. There were many unanswered questions alongside my excitement.

Aberdeen Grammar School. It was
a very imposing building.

There was one big visual difference between my Special School and the Grammar School. The Grammar School boys wore a uniform and we did not. My mother knew that attending the Grammar School was a big move in my life as it would be my first independent step into the hearing world. So, despite the considerable expense involved, she came down to Aberdeen and bought me the essentials of the school uniform. She knew it would give a psychological 'lift' to my completely new experience and would help me blend in with the rest of the school. It was the first time I had ever worn a uniform. When the children at the Special School saw me in it, they were very envious. They longed to have a uniform like mine. My mother was right, the school uniform did make me feel very grown up and proud to be taking this big step forward out into a hearing environment, despite my trepidation.

My first day there was terrifying. I had been shown the way to the Grammar School and walked the one and a half miles there alone. I felt very apprehensive indeed by the time I arrived. The school building looked even bigger and more intimidating than I remembered. Inside, an animated and confident looking mass of boys had congregated in the main hall for assembly. I didn't have the courage to join them as I knew I should have done. Seeing so many boys gathered together made me feel very small and completely lost. From that day, when I arrived at the school, I crept upstairs to the art room and waited outside until the rest of the class turned up after assembly. I desperately hoped that no one in authority would notice me or, worse still, stop to ask me what I was doing there. Despite my gruelling speech training at the Special School, my ability to communicate orally was very minimal. Luckily, I went unnoticed until one fateful day some weeks later, a prefect spotted me and stopped to talk. I could see his mouth was shaping words, but I couldn't understand a single one. It was the moment I had been dreading. I almost lost my nerve. I desperately wanted to run away. But I knew that would be worse, so I just stood there feeling threatened, inadequate and deeply embarrassed. The pride in my new school uniform and the confidence I had in my limited ability to communicate evaporated completely. Eventually the prefect realised that something was amiss and, in disgust, decided to leave me to my own devices. I was so relieved when he walked away. The boys in the school had been alerted to my deafness by the teachers but there was no deaf awareness training in those days so none of them really knew how to deal with me – or cared. There turned out to be very few Grammar School boys who were approachable so I learned to keep myself to myself. That way my solitude made me feel reasonably safe even though I was very much on the outside of what went on. Very slowly I began to discover that although hearing boys were essentially the same as deaf boys, they seemed to have a fundamentally different outlook on life, not just because they were hearing but also because their culture and experience in life were very different to mine. They came from very different backgrounds to mine. It wasn't until I started at the Grammar School that I began to realise I was relatively cocooned in the school for the deaf. There I could communicate with my peers comparatively easily through made-up signs and gestures, even though the régime forbade it. This hearing environment outside of school and home life, was totally foreign to me and presented a big challenge. I was so much on my own and often had to use my imagination to guess at what was going on. Making the connections for myself was not at all easy. Blank stares often met my attempts to communicate and it felt as if deaf people were regarded more like animals than people. I felt intimidated and very uncomfortable. Being the only deaf person in such a large, hearing school was a big shock to my system. I was considered to be the 'star pupil' at the Special School despite being quite a late developer. I learned never to try to communicate orally at the Grammar School, I always wrote everything down in what I thought was ordinary language. But even that met with some puzzlement and I often felt humiliated. I discovered that the written language I had been taught so far was very simplistic. Language at the Grammar School was far more advanced than anything I had ever known. The Principal had been right at the interview and communication did prove to be extremely difficult. It always took a lot of additional time and effort. The teachers did have a little more understanding attitude towards me than most of the boys, who never talked to me and I had to get used to being left out of things. They always wrote down everything they wanted to say to me and never thought of speaking slowly and using simple gestures. It never seemed to occur to them that I might be able to understand them in another way. My confidence and motivation sank to a very low level during the first few months at the Grammar School. It took me a long time to get to know the teachers and to begin to feel less awkward and self-conscious working with them.

The art room was a haven. I felt more at home in the spacious, bright, airy room where the Northern light poured in through the glass roof. The facilities were wonderful and I was very fortunate to have two very enthusiastic, dedicated and patient art teachers – Mr Atkinson and Mr Hemingway. During art classes, we sat at long tables arranged in two rows facing the teacher. I always sat in the middle of the front row amongst the hearing boys so that I would have the best chance of seeing what was going on. From there I also had a reasonable chance of following some of what the teacher said. However when Mr Hemingway took the class, I could never follow a word of what he said as he had a long, pointed beard which he habitually stroked and this more or less concealed his mouth. At the start of the class, Mr Hemingway or Mr Atkinson would talk to everybody, explaining what they wanted us to do and making sure that everybody understood. I very rarely understood anything of what was said to the class, but afterwards, one of the teachers would always come to see me. They would take the time to go through what had been said on a one-to-one basis so that I, too, would know what I had to do. There was no oral communication between us, everything was written down. I would then be given the necessary materials and shown how to use them. We often had to draw or paint a still life that had been set up for us. Mr Atkinson, who looked after the design and craft subjects, would then ask us to work out a design for a large poster based on our still life studies. Once again, everything had to be explained to me in writing. We were taught painting, clay and cardboard modelling, and how to make visual studies for design development work. My two days in the art room were the highlight of my week despite the arduous task of communicating, and helped me to gradually build up my confidence in my artistic abilities. In addition to the practical classes, we were taught the history of art and architecture. Unlike the visual area of drawing and painting, this was an extremely difficult area for me. The concepts that were introduced to us were often abstract and incomprehensible. The language used to describe them was far in advance of mine. But I was encouraged to try to understand some of the ideas and different cultures in very simple terms on a one-to-one basis and I learned about individual artists and architects' work from pictures. Working from a visual medium meant so much more to me. Language was still my biggest hurdle.

I built up a great respect for Mr Hemingway, who took care of the fine art aspect of our studies. He began to take a personal interest in my development and even painted a couple of portraits of me. One for my mother and the other was accepted by the Aberdeen Art Gallery where it hung for some time. He was keen to help me learn to work with others as well as on my own. He knew it would be good for both me and the hearing boys so he put me in a team with three others and asked us to design and paint a mural for one of the walls in the art room. It was a double challenge for me as I had never worked on such a big scale before or in partnership with hearing boys. But Mr Hemingway had every confidence in our team and showed us how to start sketching out our ideas. We then discussed them with him before agreeing the final design. Our sketches were drawn at quite a small scale, he showed us how to enlarge and translate it accurately on to the wall using a grid. I understood this visual system very easily. Each member of the team was then made responsible for a particular section of the mural which was to be painted in oils. I had never used that medium before but Mr Hemingway demonstrated how to achieve different effects. I can remember the lovely feel and smell the oils had – very different and new. The mural took us a long time to finish, but when it was completed it looked quite impressive and felt very satisfying. I had experienced a completely new dimension of art and felt a little less awkward in

My oil painting case, brought for me in 1954, I still have it.

working with hearing boys. As a result of my work, at Mr Hemingway's suggestion, my mother bought me a beautiful, really good quality oil painting set in a strong, metal case which I still have and use today.

As well as teaching us art during the school week, Mr Hemingway's enthusiasm led him to set up an out-of-school art club on Friday evenings. This provided an opportunity for those with a keen interest in art and design to use their own initiative in chosen individual areas. Unlike the school curriculum, it was designed to help each member explore their personal interests. It actively encouraged experiment and investigation in a whole range of areas. I was so pleased to be able to have this opportunity of working amongst people with a dedicated interest in art. I learnt a lot from

working with them and it helped to build up my confidence. As working three dimensionally was my favourite area, it gave me a wonderful chance to improve my skills. I remember building a complex cardboard model of the Castle of Mey, the Queen Mother's home in Caithness, during some of those evening sessions. Before the art club was formed, I belonged to the Life Boys and had become a Captain of one of the groups. It too, met on Friday evenings but even being a Captain didn't stop me leaving and joining the art club. Art was so important to me. I used to walk to the art club mainly to save the bus fare so that I could make a small detour on my way home to buy a portion of chips from a nearby fish and chip shop. I remember they were always wrapped in newspaper and tasted delicious.

My efforts and creative work must have been drawn to the attention of the Principal of the Grammar School because the 'trial' period to which he initially agreed, remained in operation for three whole years. During that time I came face to face with the concept and experience of exams. One day, when I arrived at school and went up to the art room in the normal way I was very surprised to be handed a set of what I later discovered were exam papers along with the rest of the class. I

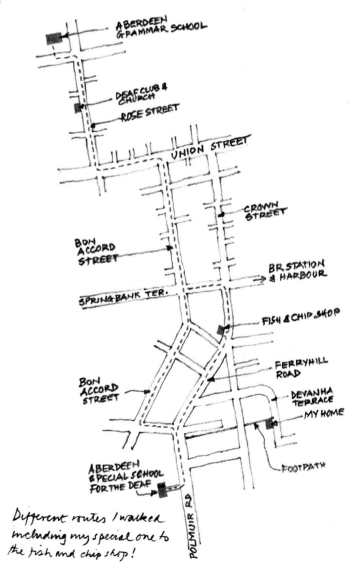

Different routes I walked including my special one to the fish and chip shop!

didn't understand why the art class had not started in the usual way. It was very puzzling. I glanced at the papers further and it began to dawn on me what they were. I slowly made the connection with the proposed Mary Hare Grammar School entrance exam that I had refused to take and realised they were to test me. After Mr Hemingway had finished handing out the papers, he talked to the class as a whole about what was expected of them. I could not follow what he said but, as usual, to my relief, he came and sat alongside me to explain very thoroughly what I had to do. There were practical and theoretical questions. The practical part consisted of having to design and produce a full colour poster. That was not a problem for me but the theoretical, history of art and architecture question was far too difficult for me because of the problem with language. However, I was not to escape the theory question entirely. My knowledge was tested by Mr Hemingway 'asking' me questions based on visual reference. For example, he would open a book of paintings, select one and cover up the caption. I then had to tell him the name of the painting, the artist and roughly when and where it had been painted. Understanding the concept of exams and beginning to see their purpose was a valuable experience for me.

Although spending two days a week at the Grammar School was broadening my education just as my mother had hoped, my experience of home life remained limited. Unlike most children, I had had to leave my home for boarding school at the age of four and had missed out on 'normal' family life. My only taste of it was during the school holidays and they always seemed to come to an end far too quickly. My mother had already seen how reluctant I was to move any further away from home and she began to realise that Aberdeen would probably be where I would have to complete my education. Once she and my father had accepted this notion, they began to give serious thought to how they might provide more of a home life for me. My father had a good job with the Post Office in St Margaret's Hope and a small electrical and plumbing business. My mother had fewer ties but they both knew there would be very little opportunity of any work, other than the manual sort, for me on the island once I had left school. To my surprise, when I was fourteen and returned home to Hameneuk for the Easter holidays, I discovered that it was to be the last holiday I was to spend there. After a lot of discussion, my parents had decided to leave Orkney and move down to Aberdeen. This would enable me to finish my education at the Special School as a day boy rather than as a boarder and for us all to enjoy some family life together. The thought of being able to live at home and be a day boy was wonderful although it was difficult to imagine not going home to Hameneuk for the holidays.

My father asked the Post Office for a transfer to Aberdeen and then went off to look for somewhere to live. He had little time to find anything really suitable so bought a modest flat in Craig Place as a starting point. It was very small, rather oddly laid out and situated above an ice cream parlour. It couldn't be compared to Hameneuk. My parents moved house when I was back at school so I was relatively unaffected by the upheaval. But it was a sad wrench for my father who had spent his entire life on South Ronaldsay and had many good friends there. My mother too, had many local friends whom she would miss dearly but she longed to have me living at home after my ten years of boarding.

Before my father left South Ronaldsay, he and my mother were given a wonderful send-off from St Margaret's Hope. He had been the local postman for twenty-five years and each of his three postal districts wanted to mark his loyal service to them in some way. A dance was held in the village hall and he was presented with the writing bureau that he still has in his maisonette in Surrey together with many other personal gifts.

Moving from an island to the Scottish mainland was not a simple affair. It involved a removal van and steamer for the sea crossing to Aberdeen. My father was sadly unable to take the contents of his workshop – the engines, generators and twenty years of accumulated bits and pieces – so he let some of the village boys come and take their pick, much to their delight. By the time my parents left Hameneuk, the Hydro Board was up and running on South Ronaldsay and had taken over all my father's electrical work.

I would have found the sight of Hameneuk and my father's workshop standing empty very sad. My memory of Hameneuk will always be as a well lived in home. The upheaval must have been quite an ordeal for my parents and I still feel responsible for their decision to leave Orkney as I know they did it entirely for my sake.

What a radical change it was to leave home in the morning and return to my mother and father in the evening! After my ten, long years as a boarder, I thoroughly enjoyed living at home with my mother spoiling me with her homemade food. This fundamental change in life-style boosted my confidence considerably even though Aberdeen didn't hold quite the same magic and attraction as Orkney. Living in a flat above an ice cream parlour was a far cry from Hameneuk but it had its compensations; there was an almost unlimited supply of ice cream as I got to know the three Italian brothers who owned the parlour. They sometimes let me help with pouring the vast quantities of milk into huge steel containers needed to make the gallons of ice cream they sold. I enjoyed spending the holidays with my parents in Aberdeen, but living in a town meant that I missed the wide open space of South Ronaldsay and the birds that gave me so much visual inspiration.

My very first experience of being close to real danger happened whilst we were living in Craig Place. I was downstairs in the ice cream parlour 'talking' to the owners one evening after school, when there was a sudden and unexpected power cut – all the lights went out. I noticed everyone in the parlour becoming very animated and although I had no idea why, I became aware of a sense of alarm in the atmosphere. A man rushed into the parlour waving his arms about, shouting something with such clarity and urgency that even I could see he was saying "Fire!" Although there were no flames visible, the parlour was immediately evacuated and as we stood in the street, it slowly dawned on me that my home above the parlour would also be in danger and my father was up there. Smoke started to pour out of the building and I began to feel

My home in Aberdeen, drawn from memory. Privet hedges were regularly trimmed by me when returned home from the south – 2/6d for my effort!

real panic. Knowing there was danger but having very little idea what was going on, made my panic all the more acute. In situations like that, no one had the time to stop and try to explain to a frightened deaf boy what was actually happening. I later discovered that, shortly after the power cut happened, my father began to smell burning. He had managed to track it down to the main fuse box, for the whole building, located on the wall inside our front door. By the time he found the source, it was a mass of flames and smoke. He ran back up to the flat to get a blanket to try to smother them. But in the few minutes that he was gone, the fire had spread so rapidly that it was beyond being contained with an ordinary blanket. Fortunately, the fire brigade arrived within a few minutes and broke open our front door to reveal my father fighting bravely against the flames in the hallway. It was a terrifying sight. I was so relieved to see the firemen come to his rescue and bring the fire under control. I was very proud of my father, but was shocked to see that his hands were burnt and very frightened by the proximity of such danger. After the fire had been put out and the building checked for safety, we were allowed back into the building. My home was a sorry sight – every single wall had been blackened by smoke and fumes from the fire. The entire flat needed redecorating.

Apparently the ice cream making process made a lot of noise which constantly disturbed my parents' life. It got so bad that, after several months of suffering with it, they decided to move. My father bought a lovely chalet-bungalow in Devanha Terrace on the other side of the River Dee and from there school was just a walk away up a long footpath. My mother became involved with the Special School and started teaching there part-time but although I was very glad to be able to be living at home, I drew the line at being associated with her at school! Whether it was by design or default, I never really knew, but to my great relief, I never had to be taught by her at the Special School – I would have had to endure endless teasing. I felt so self conscious about her involvement at the Special School that I wouldn't even walk home with her – it would have been far too embarrassing! I expect she understood that I had to maintain my standing amongst my peers, after ten years as a boarder.

My father's lifestyle had significantly changed since the move to Aberdeen. Although he had been transferred to the Post Office there, he no longer worked as a postman-driver. A transfer meant he had to take whatever suitable vacancy was available. So instead of doing his rounds in a van, he found himself working as a postman on foot doing a long, urban round. His working days were no longer spent driving through the open countryside or by the sea, instead they were spent delivering the post to a built-up area lined with houses and tenement blocks. With few lights inside the block, it was always dark and the toilets were outside on the landings. Instead of the fresh Orkney air, my father had been used to all his life, he had to contend with unpleasant 'aromas.' I often reflect on the sacrifice he and my mother made in order for me to have an education and for us to keep together. A year later, to his great relief, my father was promoted to postman-driver and to shift work.

The portrait painted by my art teacher Mr Hemingway.

CHAPTER 10

Further South

Becoming a day boy and living at home with my parents was everything I could have hoped for. Life had taken a distinct turn for the better. There were no more separations. School was only a short walk away. I was continuing with my favourite subject, art, and attending classes at the Grammar School had helped me gain confidence in my creativity. Life felt settled. However thoughts of my future were never far from my mother or Miss Jolly, my headmistress. I lived very much for the present and had little concept of the future. As far as I was concerned, my mother took care

My first oil painting, view across River Dee, when I was 14. My friend and I went by bus to Maryculter, few miles from Aberdeen.

of that. Despite my decision not to try for a place at the Mary Hare Grammar School, both my mother and my headmistress felt that as I grew up, my outlook might broaden and I might just start to understand the importance of education to my adult life. In retrospect, I was very lucky that Miss Jolly had always taken such an interest in advancing me to a higher level.

I had been studying art at the Grammar School for two years, when a newly opened, independent boarding school in Surrey, with a technical focus for profoundly deaf boys came to Miss Jolly's notice. It was called Burwood Park. She talked to my mother about it and they both thought it might be another good opportunity for me but they knew it would have to be handled sensitively. My mother made the first tentative approach; it took some while for her to convince me as I was not happy about the idea of having to leave home again or go so far South. However, I was fourteen years old by then and had grown up a little. My mother knew only too well how fortunate I was to be offered a second chance and she worked hard at trying to persuade me to think about the idea, explaining carefully that there were no such opportunities in Aberdeen and that the best I could expect there was the basic education at the Special School and art at the Grammar School. Although that was adequate for the present, it would not lead to many opportunities in the future. Slowly I began to understand my mother's reasoning but Surrey was a very, very long way away from our new-found home in Aberdeen and even further away from Orkney, and I was now enjoying my two days at the Grammar School. My mother persisted and eventually, perhaps because I understood more at fourteen than I did at eleven, I let myself be guided by her. I rose above my emotions and agreed to follow the idea of going to Burwood Park School. My mother's persistence had brought the rewards she had hoped for. She was delighted and proud of me but my decision had been a difficult one to make.

The first step was to arrange for me to sit the entrance exam. It had to be taken in two parts – written and aural. I remember taking the written part in Miss Jolly's study, sitting at her desk which had been specially cleared for me. Whenever I had been in her study before, it had always been on the other side of this very desk, which was normally piled high with papers and books. It felt very formidable. By then I understood the concept of exams and I had a little more confidence in myself. But I still felt very nervous sitting alone with the headmistress in her study. She handed me the entrance exam papers, checked that I knew what was expected of me and then left me to work on my own. Although she sat by the window, I could feel her eye on me throughout the one and a half hours of maths, English, general knowledge and simple IQ questions. I remember being very disappointed that not a single art question had been included in the paper. When the allotted time was up, she collected up the papers and explained that they would be sent away to be marked. She would let me know the results as soon as they arrived. I was more relieved at the exam being over than knowing how I would get the results!

A letter informing Miss Jolly that I had successfully passed, arrived a month later. I had been offered a place at the start of the 1955 academic year subject to my passing the aural exam. I was amazed when Miss Jolly called me to her study to congratulate me on my achievement. I had put the written exam out of my mind and had given the results nothing more than a passing thought. My parents were naturally very, very thrilled and proud. It took me quite a while to take in what passing the first part of the exam really meant but I began to understand something of why it was important and why I needed to become more independent. The future was no longer vague and intangible, it started to take on some real meaning for me. The idea of 'moving' to the South on my own was something that I began to look forward to. I had never been to England before and, was old enough to be excited about what I now saw would be a great adventure. This happy situation, however, had an irony to it. Just six months previously, my parents had given up their life in Orkney to be closer to me and now it seemed I was to be even further away from them than ever. If they had any mixed feelings about this strange turn of events, regretted their move to Aberdeen, or were worried about yet another long separation from me, they kept it very much to themselves. They wanted to support this key move in my life, whatever the cost.

I had to attend the audiology department at Manchester University for the aural part of the entrance exam. This involved a first fleeting visit to England with my mother, which in itself was a big novelty. When we arrived at the university I was pleasantly surprised to find myself amongst a lot of other deaf boys taking the same exam. What a relief it was to be able to communicate with them! 'Talking' to them helped reassure me that life in the South, as Manchester was to me, would not be entirely hostile to a deaf Orcadian boy! Mr Wood, the Principal of Burwood Park School, and Lady Ewing, the wife of the research professor at the university, were our examiners. They were both strong advocators for oralism for deaf children. Signing was very much frowned upon. When it was my turn to be examined, they each asked me a great many questions which I had to answer with my voice so that my speech could be heard and assessed. After that I was given a formal IQ test which included lots of different puzzles to solve. I found I was able to respond quite quickly to them and managed quite a high score. I passed!

Burwood Park School uniform. Never like the cap!

My education in England was to be paid for by the local authority, but it was my parents' responsibility to provide the school uniform. The school clothes list was very extensive and new boys were expected to have everything on the list. My parents had little money after their move, so this was to be a major outlay for them. How they ever afforded to buy it all, I will never know, but somehow they managed. From the approved stockist in Aberdeen, I was bought the requisite grey flannel suit, Air Force blue shirts, bright red blazer piped in gold, the school badge and the red and yellow school cap, which incidentally, I took an instant dislike to, and all the other things required

by the school. I had never had so many new clothes bought for me before. My mother also bought me a large, school trunk to pack everything into to take to Burwood Park. It must have been very good quality because it survived dozens of journeys up and down to Aberdeen and I still have it today. Being so comprehensively kitted out for school made me feel even more excited about my forthcoming move to the south of England.

The travelling trunk bought for me to go to Burwood Park School. (1955-1959) I still have it in my loft!

I was fifteen years old by September when the great day for my departure to Burwood Park School finally arrived. I said goodbye to my father and left home with my mother for Aberdeen station. We took the long train journey down to Kings Cross station in London. Uncle Frank, my mother's brother who lived in London, was there to meet us off the train. He took us across London on the Underground to Waterloo station to catch another train out to Walton-on-Thames, to my new school. It was all amazing. There were so many new and different things to see and experience. It was my first visit to London and, coming from the north of Scotland, it seemed like the other side of the world to me. Seeing the busy Underground station, the long escalators that disappeared down into mysterious depths, and walking through yet more brightly lit tunnels that led to platforms where illuminated electric tube trains drew alongside was something I could never have imagined doing. It was all fascinating and thrilling. Feeling the rush of warm air that signalled an approaching train, riding in the jostling carriage, feeling the vibration as it sped along through the tunnels to the next station, watching the doors slide open automatically to let passengers on and off at various stops was all very, very exciting indeed. Everywhere I turned there seemed to be something new to look at. It was all in complete contrast to anything I had ever experienced in Orkney or Aberdeen.

It was only a thirty minute train journey to Walton-on-Thames and then a taxi ride to Burwood Park School. As we drove along the leafy lane and up the drive to the main entrance, it seemed impossible that such a grand building set in such lovely grounds was where I was to stay. The drive was filled with parked cars belonging to smart-looking parents delivering their well-dressed sons to school. We got out of the taxi and I walked into the entrance hall followed by my mother and uncle to where the other new boys in neat grey suits were gathering with their parents. In the hall, I was asked for my name by one of the teachers who ticked me off on a list and gave me some information sheets. I stood there taking in my new surroundings. The whole place looked more like a hotel than a school to me.

Burwood Park School in Walton-on-Thames, Surrey. First floor, right window was where my dormitory was.

It had a friendly and welcoming atmosphere and I felt I probably would be happy there. The boys and their parents were divided up into small groups by the teachers and taken to look round the school. My mother was most impressed with everything she saw. I was particularly taken with the special floor covering. It looked like ordinary linoleum, but had a more spongy feel to it. This, I discovered, was for acoustic purposes, to ensure that all extraneous noise was absorbed. Apparently not even a footstep could be heard. All the ceilings were insulated with perforated hardboard for the same purpose. There were no vibrations to be felt anywhere. This was designed to maximise the use of any residual hearing any of the profoundly deaf boys might have. I was very impressed with the feel of it all. We were shown the four classrooms, each named after a famous scientist, the workshop, gymnasium and library. There were only thirty-five boys in the whole of this new school so we were to be about eight to a class. As we walked round the school in our groups, we boys started to communicate with each other and I began to really feel at home. At the end of the tour, afternoon tea with sandwiches and cakes, was provided for everyone. Then it was time for goodbyes to be said. My slight apprehension at seeing my mother and uncle leave, soon faded at the thought of my new life at this grand school.

Once all the parents had left, the Principal Mr Wood, brought all the boys together with the teachers. He first asked us what we thought the purpose of school was and then talked to us about why we were at Burwood Park. I found it very difficult to lip read him because his English lip patterns were quite different to Scottish ones. It took me a very long time to adjust to this difference and be able to follow English speech. The teachers were then introduced to us. They had all been trained at Manchester University – the main centre for training teachers for the deaf at that time – and they seemed far more approachable and less Dickensian than some of my teachers at the Special School in Aberdeen. After the introduction, we were told which dormitory and class each of us was in and which group we were to join for various activities. Each of the dormitories was named after a well-known artist, some of whom I had learned about in Aberdeen. Mr Wood went on to explain the school rules and procedures to us. After he had finished talking to us, we were sent up to the dormitories to meet Matron and her assistant. Matron was a formidable, matter-of-fact lady dressed in a crisp Red Cross uniform. She never seemed to wear anything else. She showed us to our dormitories where we were told to unpack our trunks which had all been sent to the school in advance, by rail. The same, rather ageing, but perfectly serviceable bike that my father had uniquely presented to me on my birthday in St Margaret's Hope, had also been sent down with my trunk. Older boys had been given permission to keep bicycles at school.

We were then given some much needed free time until supper. There had been so much to do and to take in and it took a lot of strain and concentration to follow what was required. We finally had a chance to look around on our own and find out from each other where each of us had come from and which schools we had previously attended. I turned out to be the only Scottish boy at the school. My new friends wanted to know about Aberdeen and the remote, windswept Orkney island I originally came from. They could hardly believe that I had come from so far away – it made me feel rather special and proud! When we went out to explore the school grounds before supper, I remember being amazed at how warm the September weather was in the south.

Supper was served in the school dining room. We collected our food from a serving hatch before sitting down to eat our meal at four separate tables. That evening, we had lots more questions to ask each other between mouthfuls. To our great delight, meals at Burwood Park, proved to be as good as home cooking. The school cook was a lovely motherly lady and very eager for us to enjoy her cooking. As she handed us our meals through the hatch, she would watch our faces to check our response to her culinary skills. That first evening, as we left the dining room after supper, one of the domestic staff, a very pretty young French girl, walked by. Poor thing, we all turned and stared at her! We were a group of lively young males who all showed the same natural instinct.

Arriving at Kings Cross seemed a very long way away by then. The other boys were friendly and I felt life would be better than at my Aberdeen school, although the first night at Burwood Park felt somewhat strange. In the morning, we were woken by Matron who toured the dormitory tapping each one of us on the shoulder – alarm clocks or bells would be of no use to the deaf. We were expected to get up at once, wash and get dressed. Then we had to completely strip our beds, neatly fold the sheets, blankets and pillow cases and arrange them in a tidy pile at the end of our beds. The huge sash windows were then flung wide open by two boys and the dormitory left to air whilst we went down to breakfast in the dining room. When that was over, we went back upstairs to make our beds. Matron was very particular about them being made properly. Everything had to be exactly the way she decreed.

During the course of the next day, we were given the timetable for the term, which was full and varied and included end of term exams. The wide range of subjects we studied made the curriculum at the Special School in Aberdeen seem very narrow by comparison. It was all rather awesome to start with, but I began to see for myself just what my mother had meant by Burwood Park giving me a good opportunity. We studied English, maths, science, art and French as well as having games lessons. It was an adventurous, flexible curriculum which was regularly reviewed and changed as necessary. Learning French, really opened my eyes to the idea that even more of the 'limitations' of being deaf could be overcome. I discovered that achievement had very much to do with attitude of mind and learning to believe in oneself. Very few schools for the deaf would have even considered including a foreign language in the curriculum at that time and, until I went to Burwood Park, I don't think I even understood the concept of a foreign language. The general perception elsewhere was that it was difficult enough for deaf children, particularly those who were profoundly deaf, to get a good grasp of their mother tongue let alone learn another language.

Good communication in English would be essential to getting on in the hearing world so speech training played a very important part in the weekly timetable. As in Aberdeen, signing at Burwood Park was strictly forbidden. Anyone caught doing so was immediately given a bad mark. My Scottish lip patterns or accent appeared to be a great source of amusement. This was something I had never thought about before. I had grown up in Scotland and learnt Scottish speech, but the school decided that it would be better for me to adopt the English accent. So in speech training classes, I had the added task of having to learn to change my short Scottish vowels to the long, English equivalents. It took a long time to do so effectively. I eventually managed it but I decided to continue rolling the letter 'r' as the Scots did. I liked the feel of it and it made people smile. So I kept that little piece of my oral heritage. To help 'correct' my accent, I had to read a story to the teacher and every time I 'mispronounced' a word, she would stop me and show me the 'correct' English pronunciation. I found it a very useful way to learn English speech, because it helped me to imagine what the words 'sounded' like. Today I still have an English accent and continue to differentiate between regional accents visually through the changes in people's lip patterns. Although it is not always possible to pick up the subtleties, I can usually sense a change in the feel of speech.

The equipment used for speech training at Burwood Park was far in advance of the balloons, spoons and rulers used in Aberdeen. There were lots of machines and gadgets to help us develop our speech. I remember one in particular that helped us achieve control of the volume and pitch of speech. The machine had some sort of bright light that was visible through a slot that ran the height of a metal tube. It responded to the pitch and volume of a voice rising as it got louder and higher. I had to be encouraged to try to raise and lower my voice which I didn't find easy but seeing the light respond to my attempts helped a great deal. Although the school was specifically for profoundly deaf boys, everyone was expected to wear a hearing aid to maximise the use of any residual hearing they might have. The level of our hearing was tested from time to time and on one of these occasions, I thought I heard external noises but they turned out to be internal and I was diagnosed as having tinnitus (a continual ringing in the head) and no hearing whatsoever in either ear. After that I was the only boy not to have to wear a hearing aid. There was little point.

Unlike both my schools in Aberdeen where we stayed in one classroom throughout the day, at Burwood Park we moved from classroom to classroom for the various subjects. Each classroom was equipped with eight tables arranged in a single curved row facing into the room, away from the window. The teacher's table was positioned in front of the row facing the window so that the maximum amount of light fell on his or her face to facilitate lip reading. As the classes only consisted of eight boys, the teaching and learning processes were considerably more intense than anything I had met with before, and it meant that individual progress was speeded up considerably. Art continued to be my favourite subject but French soon became a close second. At the start of the year Mr Clark, who taught us English as well as French, explained a little about the new language we were going to learn, and how, from then on, nobody in the class would be allowed to speak a word of English – we were stunned! But he was a very good, lively teacher who managed to bring the new, strange language to life for us. I really enjoyed the foreign words, they were completely different from English but extremely difficult to follow. I worked hard at the subject and in one end of term written exam, managed to achieve 99%. Mr Clark had quite rightly marked me down a mark for using 'sur' meaning 'on', instead of 'sous' meaning 'under'. As soon as he pointed out my mistake, I realised how stupid it was and promised myself that I would be more careful in future.

The timetable included a busy art programme but, regrettably, we only had art lessons for half a day, once a week. The art room was very well equipped and we did drawing and painting, technical drawing, metal and woodwork. However, I missed not having a second day of art. I had so enjoyed those two days at the Grammar School in Aberdeen. Boys at Burwood Park were actively encouraged to develop their creative ability, but art did not seem to carry quite the same weight as did the more academic and technical subjects. The art teacher who did his very best to help us was also the games teacher so, unlike my teachers in Aberdeen, could not devote himself exclusively to art. Luckily, I had built up quite a lot of confidence in my own work and so had some resources to draw on to help me develop my skills on my own.

During my first week at the newly opened Burwood Park School, I was voted in as the first Head Boy by the staff and pupils for the year. It came as a very great surprise and honour, particularly as I was the only Scottish boy. This meant that I wore a special badge to denote my office and had certain responsibilities to fulfill. At the daily assembly, I had to read from the Bible using my voice. It was a real ordeal during the transition of my speech from Scottish to English and involved a considerable amount of concentration on my part. As Head Boy, I was entitled to one or two privileges. One happily relieved me of having to wear the school cap which I simply could not stand! Another was being responsible for sorting out the mail every day and posting all the boys' letters on the notice board. Whenever I came across an envelope addressed to me, I would quickly finish sorting the post so that I could open it. This was a great privilege – I didn't have to wait until break to get my letters like the rest of the boys. I always looked forward to getting letters from home and finding out what had been happening up in Aberdeen. My mother wrote such good letters – I could picture everything she talked about. She never forgot to tell me how she felt my own English was improving, whether it really was or not, I'm not sure, but it felt very encouraging to hear it. Writing letters home from Burwood Park was very different from the Special School in Aberdeen. By that time my English was starting to improve but more importantly, the teachers respected the fact that these were private letters and only helped if asked. I took great pride in writing mine unaided. I knew my mother would appreciate my independence. There was always lots to tell her and my father about school and games, going shopping in the village, visits to London with the school and generally how I was getting on. I knew she could tell from my letters that I was very happy. The postbox was just outside the school grounds at the end of the lane. Every time I posted a letter home, I could picture it arriving through the letter box and my mother smiling to herself as she read it. That gave me a warm feeling and a real link with home.

At school we were divided into two houses: Lennox-Boyd, after the Chairman of the school governors and Ewing, after the professor at Manchester University. I was in Lennox and played football for my house. After the slender playground facilities for football at the Special School in Aberdeen, it was a privilege to have games lessons on a real games field. Mr Farragher, the general sports and art teacher was responsible for putting the house and school teams together and wanted

Burwood Park School football team 1958/59.
Me, wearing the green polo necked sweater.

me to play centre forward for my house but fortunately the team captain preferred me to be in goal where I was happiest and felt I really played best. We played against local schools and schools for the deaf. I remember the first inter-school match in which I played, was against Mary Hare Grammar School – the very place for which I had refused to sit the entrance exam. To their amazement, the result was an outright victory for Burwood Park – we beat them 5-0! It seemed that as we were a relatively new school, they had sent some of their youngest players, thinking the match would be a walkover. After this initial defeat, they sent teams of older and more experienced boys to matches and beat us several times but we always put up a good fight against them. During my second year at Burwood Park, we had a new sports teacher, Mr Watson, who had professional experience in cricket, football and speedway riding which we boys found very impressive. He was a brilliant player and played himself, re-shaping us into very strong first and second teams. I played in goal for the first team and remember one fantastic match we won against a huge hearing school. The local and other schools which we regularly played against began to realise that the Burwood Park team was not as easy to beat as they had once thought. The stronger teams they subsequently put together meant that we suffered several defeats but there were victories as well and I won my football colours during that second year.

One of the social activities at Burwood Park was ballroom dancing. Classes were arranged as an out of school social activity. This was something completely new for most of us and quite nerve-racking as a group of local hearing girls were invited up to the school to partner us. The classes were held in the gym and music with a strong beat was played through giant loud speakers so that we profoundly deaf boys could feel the rhythmic vibration through the wooden floor. The teacher would demonstrate the steps for the various dances and we had to follow with our hearing partners. I enjoyed dancing with the girls, but was very nervous about it. Looking back, I imagine they too must have been equally worried about having to dance with deaf boys. But we muddled through with the help of the girls to keep us roughly in time to the music and managed to learn how to waltz and foxtrot and do one or two Scottish dances.

There were links with the hearing world in the relatively safe deaf environment of Burwood Park, and we were encouraged to take our own steps into the outside hearing world. Small groups of boys were allowed to walk the one and a half miles into Walton-on-Thames to go shopping on their own. As we always went out in groups, we could keep very much to ourselves and avoid any direct verbal contact with hearing people. Communication with shop assistants was done in writing. Whatever we wanted to say was written down at school before we set out. The local people became quite used to groups of deaf boys out shopping with their written requests. It was a tidy and worry-free arrangement but did little to develop our communication skills. Paradoxically, the English hearing world was less of a challenge to me than the hearing environment of the Aberdeen Grammar School. We made a further foray into the local hearing world on Sundays when, whatever the weather, we all had to walk to the Church of our particular denomination. The English weather never really seemed cold or particularly unfavourable to me, being so used to the very severe weather conditions of Orkney and the north of Scotland. Most of the boys at school attended the Church of England. However, I went to the Congregational Church with a few other boys. Unfortunately, I had great difficulty in following the service and never really got very much out of it other than the sense of peace and respectful feeling inside the church itself.

Every term there was a half-term holiday when most of the boys went home. Timewise, it would have been feasible for me to go home as well, but the fare back to Aberdeen was considerable. My parents had to pay for my journey to and from school every term so an additional journey home at half term was financially out of the question. So, together with a few other boys in similar circumstances, I either stayed at school or went home with one of the other boys. I was rarely sorry to have to remain at school because those left behind were more than compensated by the teachers who gave us a wonderful time and took us out for treats and trips into London to see the sights and visit exhibitions and museums.

I very much enjoyed life at Burwood Park, but going home for the holidays at the end of term was something to which I really looked forward. It meant seeing my parents and old friends from the Special School in Aberdeen again. My friends and I kept in touch and would meet up twice a week during the holidays at the deaf club. That was where all the local deaf people met regularly for social evenings and events and was always very much part of my life whenever I was in Aberdeen.

My mother always made the necessary travel arrangements for my journey home. At the end of my first term, my Uncle Frank came to collect me from school and took me by train and underground to Kings Cross Station, making sure I took note of where we were going. He put me on the sleeper train ready for the long, twelve hour journey home. I remember the name of the locomotive that usually pulled the train was the *Aberdonian*. Very occasionally the *Royal Scot* would take us as far as Edinburgh where the locomotives were changed. I always knew when this happened, not because of any announcement, which of course I couldn't hear, but because of the bumping and shunting that went on in the night. Travelling home by myself in later years was very exciting and gave me a growing sense of independence. If ever I needed to communicate with hearing people, I knew I had to write down what I wanted to say or ask but I could never be certain that they would automatically respond. Some people simply ignored my written requests or glanced at them dismissively and walked by. I had to keep my wits about me and learn to persevere despite the embarrassment it often caused me and others.

I can remember the bustle and smell of the station in the evening, the carriages and huge locomotive and the clouds of smoke that billowed out of its funnel as it slowly drew out of the station. The black smuts from the engine got everywhere – my shirt collar was invariably grimy when I arrived home. I always travelled by sleeper, but I never wanted to go to sleep as there were far too many interesting things to see. I preferred to look out of the window to watch the white smoke from the train streaming by in the dark and see town lights twinkling in the distance. The wires between the telegraph poles always gave me the impression that they were waving up and down rhythmically as we sped past them. The need for sleep usually got the better of my visual enthusiasm and after a few hours I would climb into my bunk and doze off for a while. Without fail, I would be woken up at about four in the morning by a sudden change in vibration from the train. I knew exactly what that meant – we were on the Forth Bridge crossing the Firth of Forth. There was a little tradition of my own that I always kept at that point. I would get up quickly, pull on my clothes, creep

Drawn from memory. When my sleeper train went over the Forth Bridge in the early morning, I remember the powerful steel structures with twinkling lights from ships, piers and banks below.

out into the corridor, open the nearest window and throw a small coin out into the Firth for luck. I never missed doing that. Then I felt I was nearly home. There were only about another two hours to Aberdeen and just a few stops in between. A pot of tea and Rich Tea biscuits were served shortly before arriving and then I waited until I could make out the outskirts of the city. As the train drew in to the town it passed our house and, if I stood by a carriage window, I could see either my mother or father waving to the train from my bedroom window. One or other of them normally met me at the station. I was always thrilled to see them both again after three long months away. But when the holidays came to an end, unlike the return to the Special School in Aberdeen from

Orkney, I never minded going back to Burwood Park. It had a progressive philosophy that encouraged profoundly deaf boys to aim high and to always expect more of themselves. High standards were set and barriers were to be overcome. This positive attitude together with the very small number in the classes were what gave us boys the best possible opportunity in life. I came to realise that I was no longer the island unto myself that I had previously been at the Grammar School in Aberdeen.

CHAPTER 11   *Double Study*

Life at Burwood Park took an unexpected and swift turn towards the end of my second year there. During the summer term, the Principal, Mr Wood, asked to see me. He had noticed that my art work was above average and felt that it should be developed further. He wanted to know what I felt about the idea before investigating the opportunities there might be for me. As I had only started at Burwood Park when I was fifteen, he was anxious to help me make the best use of my short time there so as to give me a reasonable chance of a career. I was very interested in what he had to say, because I was very keen to progress my art in every possible way. Mr Wood felt that if I was going to make a career out of some aspect of art, I should get some specialist training as soon as possible and told me of the nearby art school in Kingston-upon-Thames. He suggested that he contact Mr Brill, the Principal of Kingston School of Art, to explain the situation and ask if he would be willing to come to Burwood Park, look at my work, and meet me. All this began to feel similar to what had happened four years before in Aberdeen, except this time it was at a much higher level. It felt very encouraging to think that my work might be good enough to get me in to an art school. A couple of weeks later Mr Brill came to observe me at work and go through my work carefully. He was to assess whether it met up to the entry requirements and must have sensed that I would be very nervous at meeting him because, when he interviewed me, he came and sat next to me to help put me at my ease. He talked to me through Mr Wood, which made his questions much easier to understand and answer. I was used to lip reading Mr Wood, so felt less on edge. I was extremely relieved when the interview was over and I was able to return to my normal routine.

Several days after Mr Brill's visit, Mr Wood came to tell me that I had been offered a place as a full-time student on the one year Basic Design Course. I could start the following September when I would be sixteen. The course would give me the opportunity of finding out which area of design I wanted to specialise in and was very exciting news indeed. I accepted the offer with alacrity. Taking up that offer, was the first major decision that I took independently. Out of necessity, my mother had taken charge of directing my life up until that point but at fifteen and a half, it was time for me to start taking responsibility for shaping

Kingston School of Art now part of Kingston University.

my own future. From then on, all decisions gradually became mine to make. Slowly I would begin to relieve my mother of this responsibility and learn to become more accountable for myself.

Mr Brill had felt I would be well suited to the Basic Design Course at Kingston School of Art but he wanted me to know that I would be the only profoundly deaf boy attending the school and probably the first deaf design student in the country. This course would provide a general introduction to a range of different areas in art and design, from which I would choose a specialism to study at a higher level. It was very exciting to think that some form of art was going to be my future. My mother was contacted by Mr Wood, to tell her of my good news. I knew she would be thrilled and her subsequent letter confirmed exactly that. Before starting at Burwood Park, my mother had talked to me about possible areas in which I might eventually like to work. At one time, she had thought that naval architecture might be of interest to me after being in contact so often with boats and ships. However, employment in that field was uncertain then. Getting a job was most important for me so the idea was dropped and the rather more secure area of conventional architecture considered. Buildings had always interested me, but whether or not architecture was to become my subject, remained to be seen. My year on the Basic Design Course at Kingston would undoubtedly determine what I did in the longer term.

Once again I found myself being the only boy going out from a boarding school for specialist education but before I could start the course at Kingston, the matter of funding had to be resolved. The local education authority in Aberdeen were quite resistant to my going to Kingston School of Art as a full-time student. They felt that Aberdeen offered an equally good opportunity at Gray's School of Art which would be far less costly to fund and would mean that I could live at home. My mother persisted with the correspondence to the Authority, pointing out how essential it was for me to continue with English, maths and speech training classes at Burwood Park, at the same time as progressing into further education. It was apparently quite a battle, but she eventually managed to convince them. The Authority finally agreed to support me at Kingston as, exceptionally, I needed the additional educational support from Burwood Park.

At sixteen, just a year after starting a completely new life at Burwood Park, further away from home than ever, I started on the Basic Design Course at Kingston School of Art. I remained boarding at Burwood Park and studied there after finishing my day at the art school. These additional studies were essential to my future in the hearing world and to my general progress. I had to have a reasonable command of language and be able to communicate orally with more confidence in order to become more independent however much extra work it involved. I also had to learn how to manage a small budget for the first time as I had an annual allowance of seventy-two pounds for the first three years as a student. I was always very careful with money, mainly because I was acutely aware that my parents had little money. It became a matter of principle to manage on what I was given. My allowance was paid straight into a Post Office savings account and after working out how much I needed to cover my bus fares, lunches and art materials for the week, I withdrew the exact amount from my account. Before leaving the Post Office, I meticulously checked that everything had been correctly entered in my savings book after any transaction, as I always wanted to know my exact financial situation.

Before I started at art school, Mr Wood carefully explained how to get there by bus. Rather than trying to communicate with the bus conductor using my then rather underdeveloped, small voice, I always took the exact fare with me and a written note that told the conductor where I wanted to get off. The bus was very full and I was conscious that using my voice at a level that would give me a chance of being heard above the noise of the bus, would draw attention to me and might well cause embarrassment to all concerned.

The bus journey to Kingston, through Hersham, Esher and Thames Ditton, normally took about forty-five minutes. It was then a short walk from the bus station to the art school. On my first

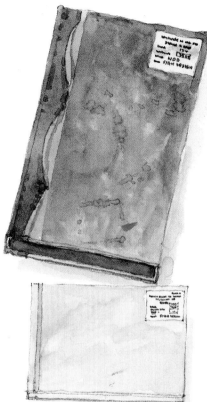

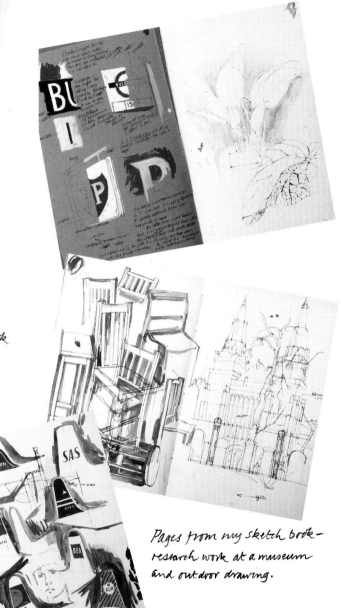

left hand page shows my research
in sans serif and serif lettering for my
thesis. Right hand page – plant study.

My examination sketch book
and thesis book. I made them
both.

Pages from my sketch book –
research work at a museum
and outdoor drawing.

day there, I was partly excited and partly apprehensive but I had a little more confidence than on my first day at Aberdeen Grammar School because I had a better idea of what to expect and had some idea of how people could react to meeting me. As soon as I arrived, I went straight to the registrar's office as I had been told, and introduced myself. We exchanged a few words orally which I fortunately managed to follow without too much difficulty. I was then taken to Mr Brill's study. It was a relief to see a face I knew in strange and unfamiliar surroundings. He welcomed me to the school and accompanied me up to the top floor of the building to meet the head of the design department, Mr Binns. He then introduced me to Mr Brown, Mr Grinstead and Mr Pavey who were to be my teachers. I shook hands with them and said "Hello" using my best voice. They seemed rather taken aback and then admitted to feeling extremely nervous at meeting me. I was the first profoundly deaf person they had ever met and they were very unsure of themselves! I felt I was at last on an equal footing with the hearing and tried to put them at ease by showing them I was equally nervous at meeting hearing people. After we had compared our degrees of nervousness, they took me into the studio to meet the rest of the first year. I was amazed to see as many as forty faces and thought of the forty new names I would have to learn and remember. I wondered what they would make of me and whether any of them had ever come into contact with a deaf person before. Would I be accepted or would I be very much left on my own as I had been at the Grammar School in Aberdeen? All the usual unanswerable questions flooded back.

I noticed everybody sit down so went to join them at one of the tables in the front of the room. It would be futile to try and hide away at the back of a group of people, much as I wanted to in situations like this. I had to give myself a sporting chance of following what was going on. The whole year was then addressed by both teachers. Mr Brown and Mr Grinstead both had English lip patterns which I was only just beginning to follow. Quite naturally, they frequently turned their heads away from me to look at the rest of the group, which meant that I could not see what they were saying. I felt completely lost during these moments but my experience at the Grammar School helped me to control my worry. There I had always been 'seen to' after the teacher had finished dealing with the rest of the class, so I sat waiting, anxiously hoping that I would get the same treatment as in Aberdeen. Perhaps the Principal had explained that communication and comprehension would take me time. If not, I would have to find some way of explaining my difficulty myself to the teachers. Fortunately, my fears proved to be groundless and as soon as they had finished their talk, one of my teachers came over with pencil and paper to where I was sitting and wrote down everything that had been said to the rest of the class. He explained that our course was mainly based in the top floor studios where we were sitting, and took me through the programme for the term adding that, at the end of each term, exams were set. Luckily these were no longer an unknown quantity to me and were one thing less to worry about. Discovering that the programme included outdoor sketching and visual studies in the London museums was very exciting as both were new to me. Previously, all my art and design lessons had been carried out in the safety of school art rooms. I was then told I would always be informed as to what materials to buy for each day. They could be bought from either the school shop or locally in Kingston. The content of each of the different components of the course would be given to me in writing beforehand to give me the opportunity of understanding a little of what we were going to do.

The Introductory Basic Design Course, similar to the art and design Foundation Year of today, was critical to any future course. If the end of year exams were failed, students were automatically requested to leave the school. The system was quite ruthless. There were few art schools at that time and places were not easily obtained. It was suggested to me, that I might like to join some of the evening classes run by the school to add further to my experience. I made up my mind to take up as many of the opportunities that were available to me. I joined several evening classes and continued with them throughout the year. An evening class in architecture gave me an ideal opportunity to find out first-hand whether or not it was to be my specialism. It proved to have too much technical content for me and I found the amount of time spent on technical drawings and specifications was rather too onerous. I preferred being more involved in the creative end of design. I led a very busy life as a student. Every time I started a new evening class it was with a different group of people and a new teacher and often in a different workshop. For my part, I was slowly gaining confidence and becoming used to studying amongst hearing peers. However each new evening class teacher was always very nervous and embarrassed about meeting the only deaf student in the school. I suppose it was only natural as people were rather unsure of how to treat me. I really enjoyed being able to attend so many classes that complemented my course. Sampling so many new and intriguing subjects was very stimulating – I had never heard of many of them before. My involvement at secondary school had been limited to drawing, painting and a small amount of modelling.

The Basic Design Course at Kingston was very hard work but enjoyable. It meant a double amount of sustained effort as my studies at Burwood Park also had to be kept up. Communication continued to be done through writing, but Mr Brown and Mr Grinstead gradually began to 'talk' to me. It was very encouraging to discover that, unlike my teachers at the Grammar School in Aberdeen who never 'spoke' to me, they realised that simple, direct oral communication was possible. They learned to face the light, look directly at me and speak slowly and clearly. It gave me a feeling of self-respect and made me feel more part of the hearing world. Towards the middle of the course, we had to decide on which area we wanted to study further. I had very much enjoyed the lettering, graphic design and three dimensional work on the Basic Design Course and asked to be considered for the new, three year Sign Design course at Kingston. It incorporated all of these elements. My request was put to the Principal and I was offered a place the following academic year subject to my passing the Basic Design Course.

The lecture programme at Kingston was difficult to follow both in content and delivery. Mr Pavey, who taught us history of design, was a very clever man and had written several books himself. Unfortunately, I found him almost impossible to lip read. He learned of my difficulty in following him and as note-taking was impossible for me, he thoughtfully started to give me his notes after the lectures. Copying them out by hand back at Burwood Park enabled me to read them at my own pace and gave me the opportunity to try to understand some of the concepts that were discussed. My fellow students were also very generous in freely lending me their lecture notes. Using the library in the school extensively helped me to gain more insight into the world of language and ideas. My deafness meant that I had to back up a lot of the theoretical course work with further research to ensure I kept abreast of things. It left me very little time for any of the usual student social life. My main aim in life was to complete the course successfully. Everything else had to take second place but I always managed the Student Ball and Student Rag Week. The Ball was always held in the fine art studios on the first floor. All the studio partitions were taken down and the entire area lavishly decorated to a theme. Designing and making the decorations for the Ball were very much part of our course and were even time-tabled in as a project. This event was my first experience of 'real' social life and meeting girls. I had never been to a Ball in my life and I was quite nervous on the night. It was a strictly student affair. At school in Aberdeen, although the Special School was mixed and I grew quite fond of one or two of the girls, there were never any end of term or end of year celebrations. Nor were there any at Burwood Park as towards the end of each term we just looked forward to the holidays. At Kingston, however, it was a very different picture. A jazz band provided live music until past midnight as we danced, drank, laughed and harmlessly flirted the summer night away. Although I couldn't hear the music, I could feel the rhythm through the vibrations in the floor. Away from the staff, the students had quite a time. The art school was transformed for the evening. One time my hearing friends and I decided to buy tickets for the famous Chelsea Arts Ball – a masked extravaganza. It was a considerable expense for students but we all wanted to see what it was like. The sheer size of the event was staggering but we were not as impressed as we thought we would be. The Kingston Ball struck us as being much more wild and fun.

Student Rag Week was another event that I never missed joining in. It was held to raise money for a worthwhile cause and involved a lot of rather mad and daring pranks by the art school students. Once I remember joining a group of students in a walk from the art school to Kingston centre. It was no ordinary walk as it was along the bed of the shallow, little river that runs past the art school. We staggered along ankle deep in the water. Some of the group found it rather cold. That didn't bother me, but I did find the stony river bed extremely hard and very uncomfortable on my feet. I previously had no idea that these extraordinary student activities took place, but I was determined to join in for the fun.

The end of term exams and particularly those at the end of the year were a considerable worry to me. I knew they had to be passed if I was to continue on the course. Fortunately, I was used to hard work and absolutely determined to make a success of the course no matter what had to be sacrificed. With a lot of extra work and despite my anxiety, I managed to pass the Basic Design Course – much to my relief, as I was very keen to move on to the more specialised Sign Design Course. By then I felt thoroughly integrated into my year group and had made some of my first hearing friends with three boys and a girl. We went round in a group and went to museums and exhibitions together and when I allowed myself an occasional evening off from my work, I went to the pub with them. I liked going out with this small group of hearing people, I learnt a lot from being in their company. My fellow students began to get some idea of what being deaf meant and how to communicate with me. Being in such a large class, it would have been very easy for me to have felt left out, but they always included me in everything and I always made the effort to join in.

The dates of the terms at Burwood Park and Kingston School of Art never coincided which meant that I often had to spend a week on my own after the other boys had gone home for the holidays. The Principal of Burwood Park and his wife, who both lived at the school, were particularly generous to me on these occasions and often took me out at the weekends. I didn't mind having to be the only boy left at school, but I was always pleased when the day came to return to Aberdeen and see my parents and my old friends again. There was always so much about my latest term at Kingston to share with them and my deaf club friends.

My independence continued to grow at home, particularly during the Christmas holidays. My father was keen to help me gain some experience of working and earn some pocket money. The Post Office agreed to me doing temporary work when I was home, with the proviso that I worked alongside my father. They were rather unsure of how my deafness might affect my work and understandably, as good employers, they did not want to put either myself or themselves at risk. Doing shift work with my father gave me my first taste of night work. I had never worked through the night before and, I have to confess, I found it a real struggle. I often felt so tired that I would sneak into the toilet to snatch a surreptitious nap, but I was far too proud to ever own up to doing so! My job was to help my father sort the post for his early morning round. The postmen energetically sorted the parcels by throwing them into the appropriate postal district bag, twenty or thirty of which were arranged in a row. They didn't always reach the right bag so I was also given the job of crawling amongst the dusty mail bags to retrieve parcels that had missed the bags. During my first busy Christmas period working at the Post Office, I proved what my father had told them – my deafness did not affect my ability or the quality of my work. Thereafter I was allowed to work on my own amongst the others and was offered plenty of overtime during the Christmas rush. I was always pleased to accept it as it meant extra pay. I remember once feeling very proud having earned £22 in a single week.

During my fourth year of holiday work at the Post Office, I was given much more responsibility. My father had long felt that I should be allowed to have a post round but once again, the question of employer's liability arose. My father argued my case constructively and it was finally agreed I should be given two deliveries a day to do on my own. It meant an early start as I had to be at the Sorting Office at 6 a.m. After sorting my delivery, I took a half-hour bus ride up to the north of the town to my round. At midday I returned to the Sorting Office to sort and collect the post for the afternoon delivery. Travelling by bus was not a problem, I had had plenty of experience back in England and I didn't even have to take money with me as the Post Office supplied their postmen with coloured, round plastic tokens for the fare.

Back at Kingston, I found the Sign Design Course had a much greater focus to it than my previous course. The content was still varied, but the different subjects – lettering and typography, shop front design, internal signing systems, exhibition panel design, different materials, graphic design, history of art, drawing and painting were studied in greater depth. I got on well in practical classes as they were very visual, with demonstrations. Drawing and painting became invaluable to my design development. Together with my visual memory, they helped to build up my confidence in visualising ideas and design proposals with a reasonable degree of accuracy and credibility. Inevitably, exams were always at the back of my mind, but by dint of sheer hard work, I managed to pass them all. Much to my surprise, I won the award for good work at the end of my second year. I continued to board at Burwood Park during my second and third years at Kingston School of Art so that I could complete my general education and speech training at the same time.

I was by far the oldest boy boarding at Burwood Park at almost nineteen. Although I was no longer a pupil there in the true sense as all my days were spent at Kingston, it was my term time home. I was fed and well cared for there which left me free to concentrate on my studies. Over the years, the school cook had developed a soft spot for me. She got to know what time I returned from Kingston and always had a freshly-cooked meal waiting for me. My weakness for steamed syrup pudding also came to her notice. When that was on the evening menu, she would make one entirely for me! I would be the only one in the dining room, and I always sat at the table under the hatch to eat my meal so that we could 'talk' to each other through it.

Despite my liking for all these home comforts, Mr Wood and my mother both felt that the time had come for me to move away and start building up my own life. My basic education in English, maths and science was virtually complete so the longer I continued to stay at Burwood Park, the more difficult any move would be. Mr Wood talked the idea through with me. I understood his reasoning and the thought of being independent and living in 'digs' felt quite exciting but I wondered how somewhere suitable could be found. I wasn't sure that I would feel comfortable having to study and live in a totally hearing environment. There would be little respite from the strain of communicating. My mother wrote to say that she would advertise in the local Kingston newspaper for a family who would be willing to offer accommodation to a profoundly deaf, nineteen-year-old boy studying at the local art school. Of the four replies she received, three looked to her as though they might be distinct possibilities. One was in London, another in Kingston itself, and the third was just a few miles away in East Molesey. She came south to visit them with me. I remember trailing round the first two and beginning to feel rather despondent. None of the houses had been really suitable and the families seemed rather indifferent to me. I didn't feel very enthusiastic about going to see the third place but to my surprise, the house and family at East Molesey proved to be ideal in every way. The house was big and very spacious, with large gardens and the room they were offering me was just right – generously proportioned with a view over the garden and my own desk at which to work. Somewhere to work was going to be essential in my final year as I would have to research and write a thesis. But the best discovery of all was that they had a young deaf son, Alan, so I would not be completely isolated, as with this family

I would be able to converse with him from time to time. I think his parents were happy that he would get to know someone in a similar situation to him. My mother felt very happy about me moving there. So for my final year at Kingston, I moved out of Burwood Park and my allowance was increased to cover board and lodging. My trusty, old bike had always been sent down with my school trunk, and this final year was no exception. I planned to cycle the few miles to the art school. Surprisingly, at that time the area was relatively traffic free. Cars were driven around at a much gentler pace than today, making riding a bike far less hazardous. I was quite keen on sport, badminton in particular, but, no longer having the sports activities of Burwood Park, I decided to join a well-known badminton club in Wimbledon. I knew I would not be the only deaf member as I had heard there was another deaf person who belonged to the club. I was quite serious about the game and played there regularly twice a week. It made a welcome physical change from the intellectual work at Kingston.

Towards the end of the autumn term of the final year of the Sign Design Course, both my teachers, Mr Brown and Mr Grinstead, and the Principal talked to me about what I might do after I had finished at Kingston. My first thoughts were to try and find a job so that I could start to earn my living and become fully independent. However they felt that having seen the way my work had developed over almost four years, I stood a reasonable chance of getting into the Royal College of Art. Rather than see me go straight into industry, they felt that a period of postgraduate study would greatly benefit me and widen my career prospects. They wanted me to apply that year. My immediate reaction to their suggestion was one of incredulity. I was almost at the end of four, stimulating but long years of what had presented me with a considerable challenge and my teachers were now advising me to carry on studying even longer and at an even higher level. I did feel rather honoured by their suggestion, it was very rewarding to think my work might be good enough to warrant a place at the most respected college in the country, but it was not as straightforward as they might have thought and I needed time to think over the idea. I wanted to discuss it with my mother during the Christmas break. I really wanted to put my skills to the test in the real world but my mother, I could tell from her face, was thrilled and very keen for me to follow the suggestion through. Eventually, I had to tell my mother that I did not want to try for the Royal College. Communication was the giant hurdle, I didn't think I could face another session at an even higher, more complex level. She was naturally disappointed as were Mr Grinstead and my other teachers when I told them of my decision. Mr Grinstead even suggested that he attend the college with me to help me with the communication side of things. I had thought it through carefully and wanted to stay with my decision despite the general disappointment it caused. In retrospect, I think I may have made the wrong decision; I regret having missed that, once in a lifetime, opportunity.

The work in my last year at Kingston was very much geared towards industry and the National Diploma in Design exam. We had to sit a lot of mock exams – far too many I thought – to prepare us for our finals. We were allowed a week for the preparation and investigation needed for the two week practical paper, but there was a great deal to accomplish in the time. Added to this visual evidence of study was a three thousand word thesis which had to be researched, written, illustrated and bound. This was a massive undertaking for me as language had never been my great strength. The title I decided on for my thesis was "Sans Serif in Motion". Sans serif is a style of typeface. I chose this because I had noted the use of a serif typeface on the Aberdeen buses and thought it would be interesting to compare it to London Transport's use of sans serif and see how the legibility differed when they were moving. I did most of my research during the holidays at home. My mother was incredibly supportive and came with me to the public library to look through many books to search out the information and images I needed. I would then discuss my findings with her in order to help clarify key points before I wrote a summary. I found it all an enormous challenge but my mother kept me going and I had no intention of giving up however hard I found it. By the end of the holidays, I had managed to put together the first draft of my thesis to take back to Kingston with me. The only concession made to my difficulty with written English was to allow for my initial draft to be read through and for me to be given appropriate language support. After reworking suggested parts of the text, I typed up the final copy on good quality grey Ingres paper ready for the insertion of the illustrated pages. I had managed to borrow an old typewriter from my digs as it was important to make my work look as professional as possible. The pages were interleaved with sheets of coloured tissue paper, something that was rather fashionable at the time. I then had to bind it myself. Although I had made and bound several sketch books for myself, I had never bound a book with text and images in my life before, but Mr Grinstead was a bookbinder and had done a lot of work for the Queen and Queen Mother. I admired his use of gold leaf lettering, which was very skillful and looked beautiful. We both knew he could have bound my thesis in a fraction of the time it would take me, but we both felt I should do the work myself. I followed his instructions as best I could and my bound thesis didn't look too bad by the time I had finished it. Having to research and write that thesis was probably one of the most difficult things I ever had to do. It was a massive struggle but it met the required standards and, to my great relief, I passed that part of my finals. I felt that if I were to fail any part of my finals, it would be this one. I knew I stood a much better chance in the practical areas.

In 1960 I left Kingston School of Art and returned home to Aberdeen to await the results of my finals. Eventually the official envelope addressed to me arrived in June. I remember taking great care in opening it and feeling very apprehensive at what I might find inside. There was a formal letter notifying me that I had passed the National Diploma in Design. I was over the moon and rushed to tell both my parents who were very, very thrilled and proud. At last their long term goal had been reached. I was finally fully equipped for life in the hearing world. All the sacrifice, expense and years of separation had been worthwhile. My mother also saw me receive the 'Best Male Student of the Year' award for a second time at the school presentation.

*My National Diploma in Design
papers – examination rules,
the notification of 'PASS' and
the diploma.*

Double Study

CHAPTER 12   *A Working Man*

Mr Grinstead continued to take an interest in me despite my decision not to apply to the Royal College of Art and suggested different areas in which he thought I might enjoy working, and where I should look for job opportunities. He knew any job interview would present me with a considerable hurdle. By then I was used to being the first deaf person that most hearing people had ever met, but meeting a prospective employer would be very different. Difficulty in understanding and making myself understood to a hearing person was not insurmountable and, hopefully, my portfolio of work would speak for itself. Being given an opportunity to prove myself in a working environment, was key to my career. Mr Grinstead was keenly aware of this and he even offered to act as communicator at any job interviews. Over the months and years at Kingston, I had learned to lip read him with ease and he had learned to understand my voice. I could not have had more encouragement from him.

Burwood Park, particularly when I was living there, followed my progress at Kingston School of Art with interest. A close link between the two institutions was formed. Mr Wood liaised with my tutors at the art school and the school governors were also kept informed. This proved to be extremely fortuitous. When it was known that I intended looking for a job in design, the chairman of the governors and one of the directors of Guinness, Lord Boyd as he later became known, contacted Mr Grinstead. He suggested that I might like to meet and show my work to the art director of S. H. Benson, the advertising agency that managed the Guinness account. An interview was arranged and I started to put my portfolio of work together.

I felt very apprehensive walking along High Holborn with my portfolio for the interview at S. H. Benson. It was one of the largest and most prestigious advertising agencies in London and I was about to meet the art director. I so hoped that I would be able to do myself justice at the interview even with Mr Grinstead there to act as communicator. Meeting new hearing people, most of whom had not met a deaf person before was always difficult. I had to be prepared to 'start from the beginning'. Embarrassed looks and blank stares usually met my initial oral efforts. It was always uphill work initially. Although my voice was reasonably well developed by that time, I knew from experience that it wasn't easy for hearing people to understand me. I kept to written communication in the hearing world for many years.

The building that housed Benson's advertising agency was impressive and modern looking. As we walked into a very grand entrance and reception area, I noticed that the lifts had been styled to fit in with the design of the entrance and were very elegant. The receptionist asked us to take a seat whilst she rang the art director and in a matter of minutes, he walked out of one of the lifts, introduced himself as Mr Ballard, and shook hands. We were then taken up to his office on the fourth floor. It was a very airy and spacious room with armchairs and a large desk behind which he sat. I had never been in such opulent surroundings and was feeling very nervous. Mr Grinstead and I were each offered one of the comfortable armchairs opposite him, coffee was served and the atmosphere in the room began to feel less intimidating. My tension eased a little. Mr Ballard talked to me through Mr Grinstead, telling me a little about the agency and the kind of work it undertook. Then he looked through my portfolio and told me that he thought the range and level of my work was good. I tried to speak directly to him myself but he couldn't understand my voice. Then the perrenial problem of everyday communication arose. Mr Ballard was anxious about whether I would manage with colleagues on my own and if they would be able to understand me.

I explained that I was used to lip reading and usually communicated in writing with hearing

Kingsway, the busy wide avenue, looking
west from Aldwych. S.H. Benson Ltd. where
I got my first job, is on the left, just above
these two double decker buses. It is now being
demolished!

people as they often found my voice too difficult to understand. Mr Ballard must have been partially convinced, because he asked if I would to like meet the head of the exhibition department. It would help me see what exhibition design entailed in the 'real world'. Despite his misgivings about my communication, I felt encouraged as we walked down the corridor to the exhibition department, past rows of designers working at drawing boards behind glass partitions. I could see visuals, mock-ups and print, out of the corner of my eye as we walked past the various studios. The whole place had a very different feel to the art school. It all looked very professional and purposeful, and reinforced my desire to get a job in design after I had finished at Kingston.

We were led into the studio where three exhibition designers worked. It was full of exhibition models and displays. I was introduced to the head of the exhibition department – Mr Ransome-Smith, a designer himself. Through Mr Grinstead, he asked me about the work I had done at Kingston and went on to explain the type of exhibition and display work his department undertook and their range of clients. Guinness was the only one I knew about. The others were equally high profile and included such companies as Lloyds Bank, P&O and BMK the wool people amongst others. It would have been virtually impossible to have followed so many new and unfamiliar lip patterns without Mr Grinstead acting as communicator. I came away from the exhibition department feeling that, despite the usual hard work in communicating, Mr Ransome-Smith had appeared very positive towards me.

We left Benson's with nothing specific about me working there being said during the visit, but it had given me my first look at how professional designers worked. I also saw for myself the type and standard of work required. I was very impressed by Benson's. With Mr Grinstead acting as communicator, I was able to both answer and ask questions relatively easily. I often wonder how difficult that interview would have been if I had had to rely on written communication alone. Back at my digs in East Molesey, I reflected on the events of the day. It had been both exciting and exhausting. After the amount of sustained concentration and strain needed to ensure I took in everything and responded appropriately, it was a relief to be alone.

Just a few days after my visit to Benson's, I unexpectedly received a letter from the art director unconditionally offering me a job. He wanted me to start work in the exhibition department as an assistant to Mr Ransome-Smith. I could start in August at a salary of £600 a year. I never imagined being offered a job before the results of my finals were known. I had to read the letter several times to make sure I wasn't dreaming. I wrote immediately to my mother to tell her and my father of my exciting news and received a long, congratulatory letter by return. Getting a job meant that I would at last be totally independent and self-supporting. I would be working alongside the very group of exhibition designers that had so impressed me on the day of my interview. I realised daily communication would not prove easy, but the thrill of being offered a job more than fuelled my determination to meet this challenge.

After the final term at Kingston had finished, I travelled up to Aberdeen to spend my last, long summer holiday with my parents before starting work in London. I remember we went on our first family holiday. The plan was to tour, driving up to Ullapool, down the west coast to Oban and back up to Aberdeen staying in bed and breakfasts overnight. In theory it sounded a good idea. But, in practice although I enjoyed my parents' company, I am ashamed to admit that I soon became bored just driving around in the car. I had not realised how used I had become to a much faster and more stimulating pace of life in the south. I think the generation gap was also becoming more marked. Long before we reached Oban, all I wanted to do was to return to Aberdeen. I felt awful telling them how bored I was, it was their holiday as well. I should really have kept it to myself, but I didn't. My parents were incredibly understanding. They agreed to cut the holiday short and my father drove us back to Aberdeen. This and several other similar episodes, made me become more aware that when communication is not straightforward, there is a tendency to be very blunt purely for expediency. I have learnt that sometimes a more subtle, but often protracted form of discourse helps to avoid hurting hearing people's feelings.

I was happy to be back in Aberdeen. The urban environment was completely different from Kingston. I spent quite a lot of time on my own painting in and around the town – there were lots of interesting things to observe. I also had my deaf friends from the Special School in Aberdeen. We played football and went for walks together. I had always kept in touch with these friends and met up with them at the deaf club when I was home from the south. It was such a relief to communicate with signs rather than in the oral way we had all been forced to use at school. Our late night, clandestine signing in the dormitories, came into its own at the deaf club.

Towards the end of July, the time came for me to leave home to start my job. With my luggage packed ready for the long train journey south, I said goodbye to my friends and my parents, promising to return for Christmas. With no more long art school holidays, I would not be able to see so much of them. This time the familiar journey had a very different feeling to it. I was on my way to the start of my working life. It was a very big step to be taking and something to which I was very much looking forward. For the first few weeks of my new job, I had decided to stay in my East Molesey digs and look for suitable, and affordable, accommodation in London closer to where I would be working.

My studio window on the fourth floor of S H Benson Ltd overlooking the entrance of Holborn Underground station where I travelled to and from my home in Redhill. It took a little over an hour.

My first day working at Benson's was quite an ordeal. I felt more nervous and isolated than I had felt for a very long time. There was no Mr Grinstead to give me moral support or act as communicator; I was entirely on my own and I would have to manage. On the way to the agency, I had to keep on telling myself to put on a brave face and tackle this important day positively. When I arrived, I initially had to go to the personnel department on the first floor. One of their staff then took me up to the fourth floor to Mr Ransome-Smith's room. I remembered the environment from my interview. I was welcomed to the exhibition department and introduced to the three designers I was to work with. Understanding them was a tremendous task as they each had different accents and their lip patterns were difficult to decipher. I quickly resorted to writing everything down and reading their written comments. This, however, took time and I could soon sense that Mr Ransome-Smith was anxious to attract my attention.

He explained that there was a great deal of very urgent work to be done, and time was money in his department. There was little time for written chatter. This bluntness was such a fundamental change from art school, that it came as quite a shock. But I was used to hard work and tried to adapt.

The first job I was given, was to design a sweet jar display stand for Barratts, the sweet manufacturers. Most sweets were stored and displayed in large, screw-top, glass jars at that time. I had to construct the stand so that it tilted backwards at an angle displaying all the sweet jars and their contents at the same time. It was quite a daunting first task. However, the design I eventually came up with met the demands of the brief and incorporated a folding cardboard support to strengthen the stand. Fortunately, it met with Mr Ransome-Smith's approval and was given the 'go ahead'. I also designed all the graphics and lettering for a range of sweet packaging for the same company. I remember trying out lots of different ideas for this job and experimenting with different

Rough sketches showing ideas for the sweetie jar stand – my first job at Benson's

techniques to get the effect I wanted. Mr Ransome-Smith always came over to my work place to talk through my ideas through written notes and sketches.

Working at Benson's was so different from working on projects at art school. There was a lot of pressure and some extremely tight time schedules. A great variety of jobs, came in to the exhibition department, from large exhibitions to small displays. Each had its own client and a deadline that had to be met at all costs. As assistant exhibition designer, I went to client meetings with the other designers but most of my work was very much of assistant nature – producing artwork for exhibition panels and helping the other designers with whatever they were working on. I was eventually given responsibility for the P&O window displays at their offices in central London which had to be changed and redesigned regularly. Working with a group and liaising with other departments within Benson's, taught me a lot about exhibition design and working with hearing people in general.

During my first few weeks working at the agency, I managed to find the YMCA hostel in London's Fulham Road and decided to move to a room there nearer to my work. The deaf world is very small and news of deaf people travels fast within it. Not long after I had moved into the YMCA, I wasn't surprised to find that a deaf boy I knew from Burwood Park had moved into a room there. Patrick made it clear that he had every intention of having a good time in London. I can remember us, once, discussing marriage and my agreeing whole-heartedly with him, that to even think of marrying before thirty was pointless. It would put paid to any opportunity of having fun. We had both had a struggle in our different ways to integrate into the hearing world, and neither of us wanted tying down. We were young and intended enjoying life to the full. He had absolutely hated school and had no interest in any academic subjects but he excelled himself in metal and woodwork and became a brilliant furniture restorer. His work was so professional that he was later appointed to look after the Queen's furniture at Buckingham Palace for several years. I was very happy at the YMCA and got to know the manager well. It was through him that I got my first freelance job some years later which involved the complete refurbishment of the YMCA building.

Life at Burwood Park and Kingston had enabled me to enjoy a lot of sport. I didn't want this to stop after I started working so I joined a social club for the deaf which had a good badminton section. I continued to play at my club in Wimbledon, but joining a club in London as well meant that I could play more frequently. Sport helped to relax my mind after a hard day in the hearing world at Benson's and I often managed to play as much as four times a week. I could then switch off from communication for a while and concentrate on the game. I was as fond of football as ever but more as a spectator and old friends from Burwood Park would meet up with me at weekends to go and watch Chelsea at Stamford Bridge or Fulham at Craven Cottage. On the way to one of these matches, one of my friends mentioned that a social club party was to be given at the Royal National Institute for the Deaf in Gower Street for all the deaf school leavers. He suggested we all went together. It would be fun to see the friends we still had from Burwood Park.

CHAPTER 13   *Lifelong Partnership*

Going to the deaf school leavers' party proved to be a turning point in my life. There were old Burwood Park friends to see and many new people to meet. As at many deaf parties, we played a lot of light-hearted games as they encourage people to get to know each other. That particular evening, we played a variation of musical chairs. When one of the young ladies landed on my lap, I felt a tap on my shoulder from the father of one of my friends sitting behind me – he signed that the girl was Scottish. I was very surprised. She was the first Scottish person I had come across in all the years I had been in the south. We got into conversation and barely had time to tell each other where we came from before the lights flashed and the game started up again. I quickly signed "See you later!" I was very thrilled to think that out of all the possible laps she could have landed on, she landed on the only Scottish one.

After the game was over, my friend's father, formally introduced me to Morag. She and I talked and talked, conversing freely with signs. It was wonderful to meet someone who also came from Scotland; we would have a lot in common. She introduced me to her elder sister, Roba, and her husband, George. They too were both deaf and lived in Surrey. Morag, I discovered, had just moved south from Greenock to live with them in order to take up a job as a senior typist with IBM in London. Although she had never been to Orkney, Morag knew of the islands and was very interested to learn that I originally came from there. Meeting Morag turned the evening into a very special occasion for me. Before the party was over, I arranged to meet her the following day. I invited her to my badminton club in Wimbledon where we played several games and had a lot of fun together. She had a good sense of humour and we laughed a lot. I wrote to my mother to tell her how I had met a lovely Scottish girl and how much we were beginning to enjoy each other's company. We saw each other regularly and a warm friendship developed between us. We met each other's friends and drifted into each other's lives. To have such a close, dependable and good friend, who also happened to be Scottish, was a wonderful thing. Communicating with her was easy and comfortable, we both signed naturally. There was never any struggle. We both understood each other so well. Morag had never used her voice because her family was deaf and had never communicated orally. They didn't use the iconic signs she and I used. Every word of their conversation was spelt out manually, letter by letter, using the alphabet for the deaf. The lightening speed at which they communicated in this way was staggering. It took me a long time to be able to follow such quick movements. It was rather like having to read animated handwriting without any punctuation. I had to rely on common sense to work out where one sentence finished and another started. (There are still a few parts of the country where finger spelling rather than sign language, is still used.)

Within a few months, our friendship deepened and we fell in love. In August, 1961, at the end of my first year at Benson's, we got engaged. My earlier thoughts of not marrying before the age of thirty had completely changed. I was only twenty-one but knew I wanted to spend the rest of my life with Morag. To this day, she still likes to amuse her friends by recounting how I never formally proposed to her. I suppose, like most young men in love, I was rather nervous of asking her to marry me. So, one day when we were in a tea shop, I unromantically and rather bluntly asked her, "When shall we get married?" I was very lucky that my assumption that she would marry me was right. I couldn't really afford to get married on my salary and Morag was in a similar financial position. Both of us struggled to live on what we earned, but we were both young, in love and would manage.

I was reluctant to simply write my parents and announce our engagement; I wanted to tell them myself. Morag understood my feelings. So we took the overnight train up to Aberdeen together to give them our news personally. I wrote to let my mother know that I would be bringing Morag up to meet her and my father. Neither of them had met Morag and only knew of her through my letters. I was convinced that my mother would think as much of her as I did, but we were both rather worried about her meeting Morag for the first time and simultaneously being told that she was to be her future daughter-in-law. I hoped it would not be too much of a shock for my parents. I needn't have worried as my mother's first question to me after she had given us a warm welcome to Devanha Terrace, was "When are you going to marry her, Hamish?" I was both amazed and delighted – it was a perfect cue to tell her of our engagement. She and my father were overjoyed at the news and hugged us both.

After announcing our engagement, the next most pressing thing was to look for an engagement ring. In the afternoon of the day we arrived in Aberdeen, Morag and I went into the town to look for a suitable jewellers. I took her straight to one of the well-known chain stores in Bridge Street. I thought their prices would be within my budget. Morag, however, didn't seem too happy about my choice of jewellers, but she knew I had very little money so we both went in. I had checked the balance in my Post Office account well in advance. It was very small so the cost of the ring would be crucial but I still wanted Morag to have the ring of her choice. Before going in, we first looked at the packed displays in the windows. Then once inside, an assistant asked us what sort of ring we were looking for. Morag told me she would really like something in platinum. As she didn't use her voice, I explained this to the assistant. I had no idea she was quite so discriminating. I thought that so long as the ring looked good and fitted well, it wouldn't really matter what it was made of. But, I discovered my future wife had very specific views of her own on the matter and I had every intention of respecting them. The assistant brought out several trays filled with an assortment of sparkling engagement rings for us to see and I was sure Morag would find one to suit her taste amongst such an array. She was however very frank with me and said that she was sorry, but not one of them appealed to her. Outside, in the street, she told me she had been put off by the sheer quantity of rings we had been shown. She felt an engagement ring was something very personal and she didn't want one that looked as though it had come off the end of a production line. All this was quite new to me. She felt we should look for a better type of jeweller. We eventually found a much smarter one in Union Street with "by Appointment to her Majesty the Queen," on the fascia, a definite mark of quality. The window display was very selective with only a few rings on show. Morag very quickly pointed to a ring that she liked. All I noticed was the price which I knew was far beyond my modest means but I wanted to please her and agreed to go in and at least have a look. I wondered how I would ever be able to afford it. We were ushered into a small room off the main shop area where two chairs had been placed opposite a small, velvet topped table and the assistant brought in a small display tray with three beautiful diamond engagement rings. They were all nearly as expensive as the one in the window, but Morag was delighted. The treatment we were given and the selection of rings were perfect. She found it extremely difficult to choose between the rings, but she eventually settled on one. It had a price tag of £68. I had to tell her discreetly that it was more than I could afford and went on to tell the assistant the same. She thought for a moment, then said that it would be possible to reduce it by three pounds if that would help. I took a deep breath, thanked her and said I would have it at that price. Morag was very thrilled and came with me to the Post Office to withdraw the entire £65 that I had left in my account. She was shocked to see how little I had in the world. But I wanted my fiancé to have the ring she wanted and, with very careful budgeting over the next six months or so, I felt I could probably manage the expense. That evening, I took Morag to the deaf club to introduce her to my Aberdeen friends and where I saw Billy Allardyce, the boy who had attempted to run away from school. Everyone at the club was very surprised to learn of our news. I explained that we had bought the engagement ring that afternoon, but as we wanted it engraved with our names and the year of our engagement, it had to be collected the following day when we were due to return to London.

On our way back to London, the train drew into Stonehaven for the usual stop. It always stopped at a few stations in Scotland on the way south. Whenever it did so, I would always open the carriage window to check where I was. This time when I looked out of the window, I was amazed to see Billy Allardyce, running up the platform to our carriage. I wondered what he was doing there. He caught up with me and stopped to hand me up a lucky horseshoe. He had brought it from his father's forge for Morag and I. We were both touched by his surprise gesture and still have the horseshoe.

The good luck horseshoe from Bill Allardyce for our engagement.

A year later, almost to the day, in August, we were married in Greenock, Morag's home town. I had taken two weeks annual leave for our wedding and honeymoon and stayed with one of Morag's aunts for the big day. Morag's brother-in-law, George, was my best man and gave me much-needed moral support. The wedding took place in St Gray's Church. It had been beautifully decorated with flowers, and the weather was kind to us. It poured with rain both just before we arrived at the church and just after we left. Out of the seventy guests, only a small number were my relations. It was too far and costly for my father's side of the family to travel down from Orkney, but I could not let my island family and friends miss our big day entirely, so Morag and I had secretly planned to pay them a special visit on our honeymoon. Touchingly, 'Mrs Mollie' and her husband, Norman, had made the journey from Kirkwall to Greenock for the occasion. She had known me all my life and was someone whom I very much associated with South Ronaldsay. It was wonderful to have someone from my island with us on the day. Our marriage service was taken by a minister for the deaf who came over specially from Glasgow. It was signed from beginning to end with a 'voice-over' for the hearing guests.

Just married!
Morag and me in 1962 outside Greenock church.

Our reception was held in MacKay's restaurant in Greenock in a large, private room. A superb wedding breakfast, splendid-looking wedding cake and countless presents awaited us. There was music and lots of dancing and towards the end of the breakfast, the time for speeches and toasts came. They were all signed but, when it came to my turn, I used my voice as well. I wanted deaf and hearing to follow simultaneously. I think most hearing people managed to catch what I was saying. When the time finally came for Morag and I to get ready to leave for our honeymoon – a well kept secret that only my best man knew – it proved to be a lot more difficult to get away than it should have been. We had retired to our separate rooms to change and just as I was almost ready, the door burst open and Morag's four, heavily built and tall cousins strode into the room. I wondered what was happening but before I had a chance to work out what was going on, my wallet, my money and our flight tickets were 'confiscated'. I was picked up, hoisted head high and carried aloft, flat on my back all the way down the long staircase to where Morag was waiting for me! I had no control over anything and couldn't even see where they were taking me. My wife of a

The 'box' toilet outside my
Aunt Etta and Uncle Jim's house.

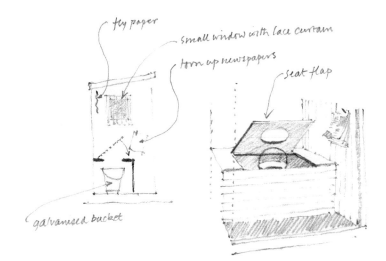

fly paper

small window with lace curtain

torn up newspapers

seat flap

galvanised bucket

few hours was amazed to see my extraordinary arrival. With much hilarity, her cousins eventually lowered me into our waiting car and returned my wallet, money and tickets. At last, we were on our way to our secret destination – a little bed and breakfast guest-house just a couple of miles away. To be on our own, was wonderful. Our wedding day had been exciting and full to the brim.

The following morning was bright and windy. We woke to an inspiring view from our bedroom window, out across the Firth of Clyde to a backdrop of mountains. The little boats moored at the water's edge, rocked about on the choppy water, their masts swaying in the wind. It was the perfect day for the return to my island.

No one but Aunt Etta and Uncle Jim, my father's brother, knew of our plans. They had invited us to stay with them but it was to be a surprise for the rest of the family and friends. Despite having left Orkney as a young teenager, my sense of belonging never left me. My roots are there. I very much wanted Morag to see where I came from and for my Orcadian relatives and friends, who had not been able to come to our wedding, to meet my new wife. We left the bed and breakfast and went by taxi to Glasgow airport to catch the small plane up to Kirkwall. This was the first time that I had returned to South Ronaldsay since my parents moved away to Aberdeen eight years previously and I felt very excited and proud to be taking Morag with me. It would be her first visit to Orkney.

Uncle Jim and my cousin Alister, met us at the airport, from where, many years ago, I had flown back to the Special School in Aberdeen. I felt so happy to be back on Orkney soil. We were driven across to Herston where Uncle Jim and Aunt Etta lived. There, we were given a warm welcome and many congratulations. Aunt Etta showed us round the house and our room. To Morag's horror, the toilet was outside. There would be no escaping her having to use it, there were no other facilities. Having been brought up in Orkney, I was more used to those sort of arrangements. My new wife, however, was very concerned.

That evening the supper table at Aunt Etta's was piled high with homemade food. Just before we sat down to this feast, a surprise guest, my distant cousin James Rosie, arrived to join us. Seeing him again after so many years was wonderful. He hadn't changed at all. His face was as weather-beaten as ever and the handshake he gave Morag and I was as strong as I remembered. I had always looked on him as a very physical and powerful man. It had taken him two hours to get to Herston that evening from the tiny island of Swona where he was the only resident and looked after the two lighthouses. The only way to and from the island was and still is by private boat and the

My paternal grandmother was brought up in this croft on the tiny island of Swona. It is now deserted except for these feral cattle.

dangerous seas between the two islands require extremely skilled navigation. He then gave Morag a package the size of a large pea. Inside she found his wedding present to us – a minutely folded five pound note. It was something very special as few people other than my cousin James would have had the strength to fold it down to such a small size.

We sat and 'talked' into the evening and James stayed with us until long after dark. He eventually said his farewells and left to make his return boat journey to Swona. The night was black and moonless and there was no light of any kind to guide him through the dark waters and treacherous currents. Morag and I were very struck by his confidence and independence.

My father had told me a lot about Swona, where my grandmother was born and where various distant relatives had continued to live. My cousin, James, was the last known resident on the island and lived there in total isolation until 1972. As he grew older, his relatives on South Ronaldsay repeatedly asked him to leave Swona and move nearer to a community where facilities and help would be at hand. Despite his advancing years he continually refused, maintaining that he preferred to live alone on Swona. His family, however, was deeply concerned for his well-being.

A perfect morning at St Margaret's Hope. You can see the pier on the right. Hoy Hills are at far back on the right. Hameneuk is in the middle, just below Bellevue.

Steps had to be taken to address the situation. There was no help to hand should anything untoward happen to him. A family party was organised on South Ronaldsay and James was invited as a ploy to get him to leave Swona. Before setting off for the party on South Ronaldsay, he set his table for a meal, using his usual newspaper as a table-cloth. The tea towels were hung up to dry and his two pairs of slippers placed in front of the range to warm. He left everything prepared for the return he never made. His family refused to allow him to return to his isolated life and he spent the rest of his life with them in the safety of South Ronaldsay.

Twenty-five years later in 1997, long after James Rosie had died, his son-in-law took Morag and I with friends across to Swona. The only life left there is a herd of feral cattle. He took us to see

Stromness Hotel where Morag and I spent the last two nights of our honeymoon.

James' house, the same house that years ago, my father had come across to wire up and install a generator. The other houses had fallen into disrepair, but James' house was still intact. Inside nothing had changed since he left for the family party on South Ronaldsay. Everything was exactly as he had left it. Not a thing had moved. The tea towels were still hanging above the range, his slippers neatly placed in front of it and his bed made. The clock on the mantlepiece had stopped and the 1972 calendar was still on the wall. Even after twenty-five years, there was not a speck of dust in sight – the air on Swona is so pure but there was a sadness to the strangely clean house.

Our first morning at Aunt Etta's was heralded with fresh tea and warm, homemade scones which she brought up to our bedroom on a tray. She announced that she would bring up a jug of hot water for us to wash with. In common with many Orkney houses then, there was no bathroom. When we later joined her in the kitchen, to our great surprise, we found the table laid for a full-scale breakfast. I tried to explain the fresh scones were more than sufficient but Aunt Etta was having none of it and we had to struggle through a bowl of porridge and a full, cooked breakfast.

Throughout our first day, family and friends dropped by to see us and wish us well in our married life. On each occasion, food appeared for ourselves and the visitors. Aunt Etta produced more freshly baked scones, pancakes and oatcakes with coffee. At lunch, a three course meal was served. It is difficult to explain the struggle both of us had to eat anything at all. This was followed by afternoon tea an hour later at which a three-tier cake stand laden with yet more homemade cakes was produced. Under normal circumstances this would have been a great treat as I am very fond of sweet things but I thanked her for both of us and pleaded with her to stop serving food. She gave us just a little respite until dinner, when lobsters, freshly caught by my uncle, were served for dinner. That proved to be the biggest meal of the day. By the end of the first day, we were exhausted and more than ready for bed. We hadn't had a moment to ourselves. Aunt Etta had kept us going the whole day long and the communication with hearing people had become a great strain for me as I used my voice for both of us. When I told Aunt Etta we were ready for bed, her immediate reaction was to enquire if we would like a cup of hot cocoa to guarantee a good night's sleep. Before going to bed, Morag and I silently agreed that we would go out for the following day to escape from even more food.

The following morning we cycled to St Margaret's Hope for coffee at the hotel but more importantly to let Morag use the ladies room. We then went to take a long look at Hameneuk. Standing there, I reflected on how wonderfully my life had come full circle. Here I was with my wife on my honeymoon. I thought back to my early days of isolation there, when I could not communicate my thoughts and used to bang my head on the wall in great frustration. During the remainder of our time in Herston we were kept busy visiting relatives on South Ronaldsay and the Mainland where my Aunts Kitty and Susie lived in Kirkwall. After that, we booked into a hotel in Stromness for two nights to give us some much needed time to ourselves. Our honeymoon so far, had been one long round of eating and seeing family and friends.

Our stay in Orkney came to an end only too soon. It had been a wonderful time. Little had changed since I had left and I felt deeply refreshed. Leaving Orkney had never been easy, but this time I had my wife with me and a whole new life ahead. We flew to Wick and stayed a night with my Uncle Douglas and Aunt Bet on our way to make a surprise visit to my parents in Aberdeen. Uncle Douglas, a keen fisherman, gave us two large, fresh salmon to take to my mother.

My mother was very surprised to answer the door and find her son and new daughter-in-law standing on the doorstep with Uncle Douglas' present. Neither she nor my father had any idea that we would be calling on them on our way back from our honeymoon. For a moment I wondered if they had somehow known we were coming because I saw there were four place settings on the dining table. However, this was purely coincidental. They were expecting two friends for the evening. A further two places were quickly added and we spent an enjoyable evening together. Then, of course, I had to make my usual visit to the deaf club.

After visiting my parents, we took the train to Greenock to collect our wedding presents, a carpet and a three-piece suite Morag's parents no longer had any use for. At that time rail passengers were not charged for taking excess goods with them providing they delivered and collected them from the guard's van so we asked family and friends to help us take everything to the station. It was quite a tight fit as the van was already fairly full, but we managed somehow to squeeze everything safely in. Twelve hours later, we arrived at Euston Station in London and unloaded all our goods. A small van, we had arranged to meet us, took us, our presents, carpet and three-piece suite back to the flat in Primrose Hill. What a way to start our married life – I shall never forget it!

CHAPTER 14

New Life: New Job

We began our married life in the one bedroomed, basement flat in London that Morag had previously shared with a girlfriend. This flat was home to us whilst we saved hard to buy our first house. During this period, I unexpectedly received a small bequest from one of my mother's cousins which, added to our savings, was enough for a deposit on a modest house. We decided to look for somewhere in Redhill in Surrey where Morag's sister lived so that we would have some family nearby. They knew the area well and Redhill was within easy commuting distance from London where we both worked. We looked at many different properties over the weekends before finding a maisonette that we both liked and could afford. It was ideal for us as first-time buyers and conveniently close to the station. Noise from the trains would not affect us and we took the big decision to buy it. Roba, Morag's sister and her husband, George, were fortunately on hand to explain the complex and lengthy process of purchasing a first property so we knew what to expect. Communication with hearing people concerning unknown areas of activity requires a lot of application and concentration. Legal terms and concepts involved in house purchasing were entirely new to me so as not to forget any of the important details, I wrote them down. Then at home I had time to go through my notes and make sure I understood them.

We were thrilled with the maisonette but the kitchen was rather old-fashioned and not at all to our taste. We couldn't afford to buy new units, so I decided to follow in my father's footsteps and design and fit some myself. I drew up plans and worked out what materials would be needed. This was where my art school training and work-experience came into their own. I bought endless sheets of blockboard and cut them down to make kitchen units and worktops, working every evening and weekend in order to get our new kitchen finished as quickly as possible.

Once all the units were built, I painted them sage green and added black formica trimmings and brushed aluminium handles. As a finishing touch, I fitted concealed strip lights underneath the top row of units. I felt quite proud of my first major home improvement and was glad to see Morag delighted too. I looked forward to my father visiting us so he could see how much I had learned from him.

Buying building materials and having to deal with tradesmen across the counter could sometimes be very embarrassing. I found it easiest to write down exactly what I wanted to avoid any misunderstanding, but found, on more than one occasion, that not everybody was literate. This made for extremely uncomfortable and difficult situations. In these circumstances I usually left without making any purchases.

I designed and made these kitchen units for our maisonette.

Our maisonette was ideal for two working people but would not comfortably accommodate the family we hoped to have one day. So I kept on doing essential work – the new kitchen, for instance, and the making of large floor-to-ceiling cupboards in our bedroom. Outside I landscaped our tiny garden to make better use of the space and the alterations stopped there.

Then, I bought a car! Looking back, I can't fathom out why, because I hadn't yet learnt to drive! However, it certainly spurred me on to start learning. After eight expensive driving lessons, I passed first time. My instructor was hearing and he made no concession to my deafness. At the start of each lesson, he would explain which manoevres he wanted me to do and then we would move off. He would stop the car, for every new instruction. He spoke very deliberately and I was able to follow him without too much difficulty. Various deaf friends who had already passed their driving test had helped prepare me for mine. I was very nervous on the day of my test, but found the examiner easy to lip read. I remember he was a very big man dressed in an ex-Royal Air Force overcoat. The test progressed in the normal way with additional stops for him to give me new instructions. I was so pleased to have passed – I would at last be able to drive my new car. Soon after Morag learnt to drive with the same school. For several days before her test, I took her round and round my test route to give her practice. She was very pleasantly surprised on the day of her test, by her examiner taking her on the same familiar route. She, too, passed first time. Having a car and both being able to drive made an enormous difference to us. Deaf people usually have to be prepared to travel extensively to visit their deaf friends as they are often scattered far and wide.

My job carried on in much the same way as before our move. But I was beginning to feel that I wanted to take more responsibility and have a greater creative say in projects. With three full-time designers in the department, there was little scope for promotion or individual development for me. Benson's had taught me a great deal and my confidence had increased considerably. I began to feel I was ready for a change so I started to look for another job that would give me more opportunities. Morag happened to know there was a vacancy in the exhibition department at IBM where she worked. I applied for it and was asked to an interview. This interview was a long session at which I was asked a lot of questions. My portfolio of work I had done at Benson's was looked through and discussed in detail with me. I was on my own, but I managed to lip read the interviewers and reply in writing when my voice was too difficult to understand. After having worked in a hearing environment for almost four years, I had more self-confidence and, this time, I also had Morag's moral support. The job at IBM sounded very interesting and I felt I was capable of doing it. Three days later, however, I received a letter telling me that, regrettably, I had not been successful. I had been placed at the top of the reserve list. If the person to whom they had offered the job, turned it down, they would offer it to me. I was disappointed, but I felt encouraged to think that I had got that far. I later discovered that the successful candidate was an ex-Kingston School of Art student and we had spent periods working together there.

My search for a new job continued. Rather wildly, I answered an advertisement for an 'imaginative draughtsman' at the London County Council (LCC) not having much idea of what the work would involve. I thought it might possibly give me a little more scope than my present job. To my surprise, I was asked to attend an interview. It was far more formal than any of the previous ones, with five men sitting on the panel. However, I felt fairly confident and was not to be daunted. I honestly can't imagine how I ever dealt with so many different hearing people asking me questions. When I think back to that interview, it is a mystery to me how I got through almost entirely orally. Only four years previously in my first job interview, I would have got hopelessly lost with the communication without the assistance of Mr Grinstead. Halfway through the interview, the chairman of the panel astonished me by saying there was, in fact, another vacancy for a qualified designer in another section and asked if I would be interested in it. This section was responsible for most of the publicity and exhibition design for the LCC. I was amazed that by applying for a job that I wasn't too sure about, I had stumbled across exactly the kind of job I really wanted. I indicated my interest immediately.

David Siegle-Morris, the head of the furniture and display section, came down to look at my portfolio of work. He showed a genuine, open and considerate attitude towards me and after he had finished asking me questions about my current work and had looked through my portfolio, he turned to me and simply asked if I would like to start work in the display group in his section as an exhibition and graphic designer the following week. I couldn't believe my luck, even the starting salary was to be considerably higher than at Benson's where I had been for the last four years. Not only would the type of job be far broader and entail more responsibility, it would also have good long term prospects. I went home, almost walking on air, to tell Morag of my good fortune. She was very thrilled and proud of me. This move would make a significant difference to us.

The following Monday, I was to report to Ken Mellor, the head of the display group at County Hall. The group I was to work with, was located on the sixth floor of County Hall's new extension. The County Hall is an enormous and imposing building on the South Bank of the River Thames, next to Westminster Bridge. Ken Mellor, who was also a well-known set designer, greeted me warmly. He then introduced me to the other designers and suggested I spend the day getting the feel of the group, talking to them and looking through some of their work. I found the work very interesting and stimulating and far more wide-ranging than anything I had so far been involved. I felt I would really enjoy working alongside such interesting and creative people.

Working with my new hearing colleagues meant that as well as my adjusting to them, they also had to adjust to me. As I came to rely less on written communication and more on speech, they had to learn not to mumble, look away or turn their backs to me when talking to me. I had to be able to see their faces clearly through any conversation and they would need to make a point of facing the light. I was briefed for my first job by Ken Mellor. He carefully explained that the Royal

My work place at the County Hall,
London – a long way from Orkney!

Festival Hall was to be extended and refurbished and that I was to be responsible for designing the internal signing system. I was given plans for the complex and shown where the signs were to be sited. I studied them in depth before going out on site with the job architect. The entire building was in a state of disruption. Scaffolding and workmen were everywhere. There were piles of rubble from the basement to the top floor. We picked our way through them so that I could get sight of where the signs had to go. I had to use my imagination quite a lot as the building was in such a mess, but I felt very excited at undertaking the job on my own. Working on the signs proved to be

Rough sketches for the Royal Festival Hall (London) signing system, I designed.

extremely interesting and involved making many of my own creative decisions, something that I had very much looked forward to doing. I learned a considerable amount about signing systems from Harry Hooper, the signs expert. He was also the man responsible for all the immaculate lettering on London's historic blue plaques.

I continued to commute to work by train from Redhill and, over the years, got to know several of my fellow travellers. The journey only took half an hour or so, but I always kept a look out for people I knew on the platform so as to avoid habitually sitting next to them. Doing so invariably meant them feeling the need to make conversation with me which was difficult against the noise of the train. Oral communication in any noisy environment is always difficult and embarrassing because of my small voice. In those situations, I try to keep myself to myself. For probably similar reasons, hearing people I knew, would sometimes deliberately avoid me. I remember one incident, when the minister from a local Church was waiting for a train on the same platform as me. I looked towards him and, as soon as he caught my eye, he looked straight past me and walked purposefully away in the opposite direction. I knew he probably didn't want the effort of talking to me, but I nevertheless, felt very uncomfortable and a little hurt. There were and still are often instances where people shy away from my deafness and my voice. I had to learn to ignore these reactions. Deafness has no outward symbol and hearing people are apt to misinterpret the unfamiliar speech of deaf people. If they do realise deafness is the problem, I notice they often shout very loudly, attracting stares from other people and it is extremely embarrassing. The invisibility of deafness can also lead to very uncomfortable misinterpretations of situations. Travelling home from work, I would sometimes fall asleep on the train. On one occasion, I was woken by a sharp, painful kick in the ankle. The passing ticket collector had apparently asked to see my ticket. As I couldn't hear him and carried on sleeping, he had wrongly assumed I was trying to deceive him. My regular fellow travellers were clearly outraged at this incident.

Commuting by train could sometimes turn into something of a challenge. When delays, cancellations, rail works, or any change to the timetable were announced over the public address system, I couldn't hear them. Waiting for a train home from London after work, amongst the huge crowd of people who were all checking the departure board for platform information, I would suddenly see a large section of the crowd hurrying across the concourse in a particular direction. There was no apparent reason or change on the information board. I came to know this behaviour had probably been caused by a loudspeaker announcement which, as far as I was concerned, could have been about something as serious as a bomb scare, or as straightforward as a change of platform. The unknown was always a worry to me. I felt helpless. Relying entirely on the information board did not guarantee accurate information and many times I would end up at a totally unexpected destination. I always tried to look out for people whom I knew travelled to Redhill regularly, and then follow them.

During my first year with the display group, owing to local government reorganisation, the London County Council became the Greater London Council. The display group was given the brief for an exhibition to explain the history of the LCC and the changes that becoming the GLC would mean. It was to be a big and comprehensive exhibition spread over five rooms involving a lot of work and a very tight time schedule. Two of the rooms were my responsibility. As a group, we spent many long evenings working late into the night to complete the exhibition in time for the official opening by the Queen. On the day, the design team were lined up to meet her. She stopped and shook our hands. I felt very honoured. I had only ever seen her on the television before and hadn't realised quite what a small lady she was.

In the early Spring of 1965, life at home in Redhill changed dramatically. I had been given a considerable rise in salary, so Morag and I decided to start the family we had wanted. Soon Morag told me she was expecting our first baby. I felt very proud and excited at the prospect of becoming a father. Both our parents were equally thrilled at becoming grandparents and the following November Fiona was born. Our greatest surprise was that our baby daughter was born hearing. We were both very happy yet anxious about how we, as deaf parents, would manage to bring her up appropriately. Having a hearing baby was probably as baffling to us as hearing parents having a deaf baby. Morag was determined to find ways of making sure Fiona had plenty of contact with hearing people. She also knew that Fiona would need her support in the hearing world. As Morag had never used her voice, any communication with the hearing world on her daughter's behalf, would be totally reliant on signing and written notes. So to give Fiona the support she would need, Morag bravely decided to learn how to use her voice. The search for a speech therapist was long and arduous and all she could find, was someone who was willing to work with her for a mere half an hour a week. But with a lot of dedication and commitment, she made a success of it.

Our doctor advised us to take Fiona to a full-time nursery school to help her adjust to other hearing children and experience a hearing environment on a regular basis when she was nine months old. We were unable to help her in that way at home and accepted that Fiona would have to have external support. She grew into a very bright and sharp little girl. I remember her hearing a tap dripping, going to see where the sound was coming from and then coming to tell me to turn it off! To be made aware of sounds in the house was a very new and different experience for us.

As the work of the GLC began to expand, so did the display group and sometime later, Maggie's husband, Bob – a graphic designer, joined us. Colleagues and each of the new members of the group, learned to attract my attention by tapping me on the shoulder, waving at me or stamping on the floor. Stamping on the floor was a simple and effective way of attracting my attention, providing the floor was wooden. Sometimes outside the studio, one of them would forget and accidentally, ineffectively and painfully stamp on a concrete floor! Communication became less and less of a struggle as I used my voice more and more. In the early days when Bob first joined the group, I remember him trying to explain something to me and us both getting very confused. He started to write his explanation down. I gently stopped him. By then I was determined to rely on oral communication as much as possible and only resort to writing things down if all else failed. Persevering in this way and working in an understanding environment, made me feel almost as though I was hearing myself. Instead of always having to speak to my colleagues face to face, I was able to tap them on the shoulder, use my voice to speak to them whilst they carried on working, and see them respond by nodding or shaking their head. It was a wonderful feeling to feel so much part of this group. I was surprised to observe how easily hearing people were distracted in the work place. Not being aware of aural disruptions, I was able to concentrate on my work. I even gained a reputation for 'churning' work out, which amused me. We worked well as a team, shared a similar sense of humour and had a lot of fun. We frequently had lunch together in the County Hall restaurant overlooking the Thames. My colleagues always included me in what they did and became my first lifelong hearing friends – Bob, Keith, Birgit and Mac.

Maintaining my independence as a designer at the GLC was most important to me. I was happy to work in partnership with my colleagues, but was determined never to become reliant on any one of them. There were, however, instances when, as part of the team, a colleague would accompany me to briefings and meetings to assist with the communication if necessary. I was very appreciative of the extra time and effort put in by them on my behalf and never took it for granted. This support contributed to my being able to take on projects myself. Whilst reminiscing with Bob about our days at the GLC and discussing the general difficulties of getting a good, clear design brief from a client, I came to realise how much more preparation my clients took knowing of my deafness. My colleagues were always amazed at how well prepared the various clients and contractors were for me in contrast to them. This underlined my observation that quick and easy verbal dialogue did not necessarily guarantee good or accurate communication. I realised that, perhaps, I had an advantage over hearing people in these instances.

One particular difficulty I did have was not being able to use the telephone. I never liked asking colleagues for favours, but when it came to the telephone, I had no option. I was very grateful that my wanting to be on an equal footing with my hearing colleagues was respected in the group.

Using the telephone system was not always to be such a barrier for deaf people. An early system, using modified, redundant GPO teleprinters, was developed. These early, cumbersome, paper-based machines were superseded by the neat Minicom 'telephone' used today which incorporates a keyboard, an acoustic coupler for the telephone receiver and a small visual display unit for incoming 'calls' and outgoing messages. It was a real breakthrough. I remember the thrill I felt the first time I 'spoke' to Bob and Maggie via Minicom. When fax machines came on to the market,

Morag using one of early telephone for the deaf.

communication between deaf and hearing people and between deaf people themselves was transformed almost overnight. Life took on a whole new dimension.

Two years after Fiona was born, a second child was on the way and the following May, Morag went into hospital to give birth to our second daughter, Morna. Like her older sister, she too, was born hearing. We were thrilled. Our daughters would have each other to talk to and learn from and we would help them to understand the deaf world. The day Morna was born was, however, to have a bitter twist to it. Only a few hours after welcoming our new baby into the world, the results of a post-measles test came through for little Fiona. She had contracted it a few months earlier, recovered and returned to her normal routine at nursery school within a few weeks. However, she did not seem quite so alert as usual. Morag took her to the doctor and he arranged for her to see an audiologist to have a hearing test and now we knew the outcome . . . she had suffered a severe loss of hearing and was virtually deaf. It was so hard – we felt desperately sorry for her. Our only compensation was that deafness, was a well-known quantity to us. We knew the pitfalls and most of what there was to know about being deaf. Furthermore, by this time, people were more aware of deafness and its implications. The deaf were no longer regarded as outcasts. New technological developments had made considerable inroads into communication for the deaf since our childhoods.

Over the years, we came to have complete trust in both our daughters and they

My home in Redhill, a semi detached house, on the left side.

instinctively took communication responsibilities from a very early age. Fiona has been able to interpret for us when necessary and Morna has been able to facilitate me using the telephone at home since she was six years old. However, as deaf parents of a hearing daughter, we were always very careful never to put her under any pressure. When Bob sometimes had to contact me at home, Morna would answer the phone, listen carefully to what he said and then fetch me and sign the message to me. These messages sometimes involved quite complex matters relating to work. She would wait for me to sign my reply and then relay it verbally over the phone back to Bob.

Our maisonette soon became too cramped for our growing family and we moved to a semi-detached, three-bedroomed house with a garage and garden. Once we had moved in and were enjoying the extra space, we began to find several things wrong with it. The fuses blew every time we switched on anything electrical. It was obviously not safe. Knowing of my father's electrical enterprises in Orkney, I wrote to ask him for advice. He was concerned about this state of affairs and suggested he and my mother came down to Redhill for two weeks. He knew that, after the expense of moving house, we would have very little left for this essential work and he offered to rewire the whole house himself. Working as his assistant, under his instruction, I helped strip out the old system. My father and I have a close affinity which has helped to facilitate communication between us. He has never used any signing, we have always talked to each other as a hearing father and son would. His gestures and animated face lend colour and depth to his speech. I lip read him easily. He worked day and night and completed the rewiring almost within the first week of his stay. It probably took him back to his early days when he supplied power to houses in St Margaret's Hope.

I gained more confidence in undertaking large household jobs after having worked on the rewiring with my father. The plumbing was in a dreadful state. It could take up to half an hour to fill the bath. So I took myself off to the local library to find all the books I could on plumbing. Without my mother's early insistence on making me understand the value of reading, I would probably not have thought of doing this. At the time, I could not see how it could ever be useful to me, but I was made to persevere. With the knowledge gained from the library books, I stripped out all the old pipe work, replaced it with new copper piping and put in a new hot water tank. It was a very big job and took me many evenings and weekends. On the day I apprehensively turned on the water, I was amazed to find everything worked and there was not a drip or leak in sight!

The kitchen in our new house was old and in a poor state. With the experience I had gained from putting in a new one in our maisonette, I embarked on a more ambitious layout. With two children to keep an eye on around her and one of them deaf, communication for Morag would be an important factor in this kitchen design. She would need as much vision as possible. To address this, I built a central island to take the sink. When others were in the kitchen, it allowed Morag to communicate with greater ease. I recently came across an article in a magazine for the deaf, praising the design of a kitchen with an island sink in it and discovered that it was based on my design.

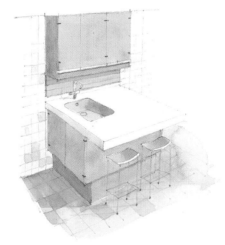

My personally designed and built Kitchen sink 'island' unit.

CHAPTER 15　　*Full Circle*

When Morna was still a baby, two teachers for the deaf came to us for advice. They had unusually come to realise that, without personal knowledge of how to communicate effectively with deaf children, they could not teach them with any degree of success. For the first time in our lives, we were being asked to help facilitate the work of two hearing, professional people by sharing our experience of being deaf. It was the start of a wonderful partnership between deaf and hearing people and became the foundation of what were to become two organisations promoting the integration of deaf and hearing people.

After meeting these two teachers, Morag and I decided, together with our deaf friends, to form the Breakthrough Trust to provide an integrated opportunity for deaf and hearing families to get together at organised social, sports and fund-raising events. We would always take Fiona and Morna with us to these events, as we wanted them to gain experience outside the deaf family home and mix with other deaf and hearing people as early as possible. We were determined to prevent them becoming insular. Morag became the part-time officer for communication through sport and organised many events. I also ran several painting weekends which gave me an opportunity to share one of the activities I enjoy most with other interested people.

Having a hearing child in the family had made Morag and I realise just how isolated from the hearing world we and other families were – deaf mothers in particular. Similarly hearing mothers with deaf children would be isolated from the deaf world. Our own deaf and hearing family became the inspiration for Morag to, independently from Breakthrough, set up an organisation to provide opportunities for young people to meet successful deaf people. From these role models, youngsters could learn, first hand, how it was possible to gain confidence and become deaf high achievers integrated into a predominantly hearing world. Her move was visionary to me. Not only did it nurture and encourage self-worth and esteem in young deaf people, it also enabled Morag and I to purposefully feed our own life experience back into deaf and hearing families. Morag and her early organisation had my full and active support as it grew into the national charity, 'Friends for Young Deaf People – a unique partnership between deaf and hearing people.' FYD, as it is generally known, went from strength to strength with Morag first as chairman, then director, and finally as president. It has provided a springboard to successful lives for countless young deaf people. I was filled with unbelievable pride when in 1995 she went to Buckingham Palace to receive an MBE from the Queen for her services to young deaf people.

I now have time to return to Orkney for family events and holidays. All my visits are memorable but the one I made with my father to attend my Aunt Kitty's funeral a few years ago stands out in my mind. On the day of the funeral the undertakers took the coffin to the little church at Eastside and after the service finished, we pallbearers carried the coffin out to the graveside. I stood up to take my place with the five other men and bent down to take one of the ornate brass handles on the side of the coffin. As I put my hand round it I noticed it was not the beautifully moulded brass handle it appeared to be. It was in fact a pressed version with extremely sharp edges that began to dig painfully into my hand as we took the weight of the coffin and carried it out of the church into the cemetery to the freshly dug grave where she was to be buried. At the graveside the undertakers gave each of the pallbearers the end of a rope, which passed under the coffin to those on the opposite side in order to lower it in a slow and dignified manner into the ground. I think I was standing at the end of the coffin opposite Doug, my cousin's husband. As we held the ropes tightly and lifted the coffin over the grave, we held it there while the minister said the commital and quite suddenly, without warning, I felt a sharp tug and the rope tighten round my hand as I was jerked to the edge of the grave. The other five pallbearers had released their ropes to lower the coffin. As I struggled to get my balance and my hand free I noticed the coffin suspended at a 45 degree angle because I was still grimly holding the rope! I was on the verge of panic when I realised that the minister must have asked at some point, during or after the commital, for the coffin to be lowered and of course I would not have heard! Eventually I managed to work my hand free from the rope to allow the coffin to come to its resting place – if at a rather unusual angle! I was acutely embarrassed though no harm was done and both my father and I saw the funny side of the incident.

Eastside Parish Church, where past generations of the Rosies are buried. The insert shows a detail of a gravestone next to where my grandparents and Aunt Susie are at rest.

This particular visit gave my father the opportunity to return to his native Orkney after more than thirty years absence. In 1972, Morag and I were sitting at home watching television when the door bell rang and the lights flashed. We were both taken by surprise as it was late and we were not expecting anybody. I knew it was likely to be a stranger. I went to answer the door and, to my disbelief, saw what looked like the familiar silhouette of my father's figure through the reeded glass panels. When I opened the door, I found it was indeed him standing on the doorstep with a suitcase! I was baffled – what was he doing here unannounced? There had been no mention of his coming south in any letter. He said he would explain once he was inside. We then learned that he and my mother had finally decided to leave Scotland to come and live to be near us. They had even sold their house in Wick to do so! My father had come to stay with us in order to find somewhere to live in Redhill before my mother joined him. It all seemed impossible to us! We were of course pleased for them, but very concerned about them having left all their friends behind in Aberdeen. My father, however, was convinced that he and my mother would make plenty of new friends through the church in Redhill. He had obviously thought everything through and within a few months he managed to find a maisonette. They started their life in the south just a short distance from us. Since her death in 1988, my father has lived alone in the same maisonette – at over ninety, he is as independent as ever.

I still live in Redhill with Morag and my family near by. With both daughters married we are grandparents three times over. I count my blessings. Events could have, so easily, been very different. Looking back over my life, I often reflect how, without my mother's indomitable spirit and vision, I could well have been relegated to a life of obscurity and loneliness. Without my father's example of ingenuity and application, I may not have developed my own work ethic and sense of worth. I will always be grateful for the kindness and support given to me by countless hearing and deaf people who have recognised that communication is not so much a problem as an attitude of mind. Since retiring in 1990, besides forming Gordon Rosie Partners with Bob and Maggie, I have set aside time to develop my passion for painting. The security, beauty, freedom and spiritual well-being that come from my island continue to inspire me to draw and paint.

Looking out from my island.

Author's Postscript

Over the years I have thought deeply about what Hamish's outwardly soundless life means and the amazing way that he has managed to break through so many barriers. It was this thinking that eventually formed the proposal for my Masters' degree at Edinburgh College of Art when I was working there as Course Leader in the Visual Communication department. It gave me an ideal opportunity to look deeply into the silence and apparent limitations of deafness and to research possible ways of visualising the feel of everyday sounds for an audience that has no knowledge or memory of sound. Hamish and others proved to be very useful 'sounding boards' for ideas in an area where little visual work had been undertaken. I could only begin to imagine the challenge of life for Hamish without the communication technology or interpreting services for the deaf that exist today. Research is never easy, but my intrigue with Hamish's remarkable achievement drove me on. I remember one particular day when I felt I had finally gone some way to visually resolving how the sound of a 'whisper' and a 'laugh' might feel to a profoundly deaf person. I faxed my ideas to Hamish. His response read simply, "Marvellous ideas, now I can 'hear' what you mean! love, Hamish" His directness was rewarding and I felt delighted that my notion, that letters and colours could be used inventively to capture the feel of basic sounds for the profoundly deaf, had been vindicated. I began to see the way ahead that led to my illustrated thesis finally gaining recognition by way of a Masters' degree in 1993.

Having seen my interest in visual communication, Hamish and Morag wanted me to learn sign language and invited me to various publicly signed events to introduce me to the idea. The most magical and persuasive of all was a signed Christmas carol concert in London. That evening, I met Hamish and his family at St Paul's Church in Knightsbridge where a large, illuminated Christmas tree stood outside, swaying in the breeze. Inside the church, the atmosphere was warm and alive with people signing animatedly to each other. Hamish came to greet me and show me to the seat he had reserved for me at the front so that I would see as much of the signing as possible.

The service started and the hearing and signing choirs took turns to perform traditional and modern carols. It was a new, and a fascinating experience for me. I turned to see Hamish and his family, along with many others in the congregation, signing the words along with the choirs, their faces alight with the pleasure of joining in. They could 'see' the carols and music and feel them through sign language, even though they could not hear the singing choir. It was very moving. As someone involved in the art of graphic communication, I was able to see for myself the breadth and depth of access that sign language could give and found an added, visual dimension to oral and written language. I was so inspired by that evening that I decided I would start learning sign language, with a very particular aim. I wanted, one day, to be part of a signing choir. It took commitment and perseverance on my part and a great deal of patience and encouragement of several dedicated sign language teachers to help me achieve my aim three years later. Being able to communicate both the spirit and the words of the carols to Hamish, his family and the deaf-hearing congregation was a very special experience for me and gave me some insight into his world.

I have learned much from writing Hamish's story. It has taken both of us many, many hours of meetings and I have had to ask him innumerable questions, followed up by more queries and informed attempts at some of his deeper, more hidden feelings. In his meticulous cross checking of my writing, he has generously commented that he wonders how I could have known his feelings. It was because his communication in telling me his story was so total – oral and signed which included meaningful facial expression and body language which, combined with my knowledge of sign language, helped me to read 'between the lines'.

From reading the latter part of Hamish's story, one might think that he was lucky to have found himself working amongst a group of such supportive hearing colleagues in the display group at the GLC. Up to a point, that is true, but Hamish has always made a substantial contribution to making opportunities work for him. His positive attitude, good humour, resilient disposition and enthusiasm are contagious. They make people want to take time and make the effort to communicate with him and continue to bring him well-deserved reward and recognition.

Maggie Griffin